Contemporary's
NUMBER POWER

Word Problems

KENNETH TAMARKIN

Project Editor:
Ellen Frechette

Consultants:
Michael Dean
Elizabeth Shaw
VTAE—Adult H.S. Program
Broward County, Florida

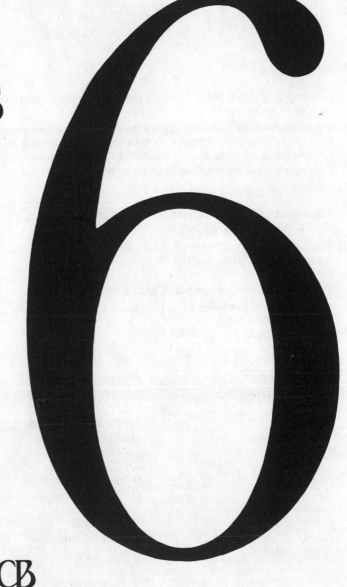

CB
CONTEMPORARY
BOOKS
CHICAGO

Library of Congress Cataloging-in-Publication Data

Tamarkin, Kenneth.
        Number power 6 / Kenneth Tamarkin. — Rev. ed.
            p.   cm.
        ISBN 0-8092-4024-6
            1. Word problems (Mathematics)   2. Problem solving.   I. Title.
        II. Title: Number power six.
        QA63.T36   1990
        513—dc20   90-2544
                                                                                                          CIP

Published by Contemporary Books, Inc.
Two Prudential Plaza, Chicago, Illinois 60601-6790
Manufactured in the United States of America
International Standard Book Number: 0-8092-4024-6

Published simultaneously in Canada by
Fitzhenry & Whiteside
195 Allstate Parkway
Markham, Ontario L3R 4T8
Canada

Editorial Director
Caren Van Slyke

Editorial
Kathy Osmus
Christine Benton
Lisa Black
Janice Bryant
Karin Evans
Eunice Hoshizaki
Robin O'Connor
Karen Schenkenfelder
Debbie Weiner

Editorial Production Manager
Norma Fioretti

Production Editor
Jean Farley Brown

Production Assistant
Marina Micari

Art & Production
Princess Louise El
Ophelia M. Chambliss-Jones

Typography
Terrence Alan Stone

Contents

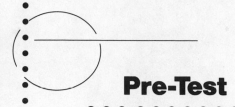

Pre-Test

For all problems, circle the letter of the correct answer. Round off decimals to the nearest penny or the nearest hundredth.

1. 1,600 pounds of steel are used to make a Chevrolet. The automobile plant produced 840 Chevrolets in 1 day. How many pounds of steel were needed that day to make the cars?

   a. *2,440 pounds*
   b. *1,344,000 pounds*
   c. *760 pounds*
   d. *244,000 pounds*
   e. *none of the above*

2. In 1 year, Melinda grew $2\frac{1}{4}$ inches to $48\frac{3}{8}$ inches. What was her height at the beginning of the year?

   a. *$50\frac{5}{8}$ inches*
   b. *$46\frac{1}{8}$ inches*
   c. *$43\frac{1}{2}$ inches*
   d. *$21\frac{1}{2}$ inches*
   e. *$108\frac{27}{32}$ inches*

3. Cynthia took 19 girls roller-skating. If it cost $.75 for each of the children to get in and $.50 for each of them to rent skates, how much money did Cynthia have to collect?

   a. *$20.25*
   b. *$23.75*
   c. *$17.75*
   d. *$1.25*
   e. *$4.75*

4. During the big spring sale, Jean bought a coat for $79.50, which was 75% of the original price. What was the original price of the coat?

   a. *$106.00*
   b. *$59.63*
   c. *$154.50*
   d. *$94.34*
   e. *not enough information is given*

5. Diana makes lemonade from the powdered concentrate by combining 5 tablespoons of concentrate with 2 cups of water. The directions say you should use 24 cups of water for the entire container of concentrate. How many tablespoons of concentrate are in the container?

   a. 240 tablespoons
   b. 130 tablespoons
   c. 110 tablespoons
   d. 60 tablespoons
   e. 31 tablespoons

6. Carol was told that she would have to pay $684 interest on a $3,600 loan. What interest rate would she have to pay?

   a. $2,912
   b. $4,284
   c. 19%
   d. 5.3%
   e. 81%

7. Jack bought a turkey for $8.34 and a chicken for $4.17. How much did he spend on the meat?

   a. $2.00
   b. $4.17
   c. $12.51
   d. $34.78
   e. $20.00

8. The New Software Company received a shipment of 200,000 foam pellets to be used in packing boxes. If New Software uses on the average 400 pellets for each box, how many boxes can be packed using the shipment of pellets?

   a. 2,000 boxes
   b. 800 boxes
   c. 199,600 boxes
   d. 80,000,000 boxes
   e. 500 boxes

9. Oranges cost $1.50 a dozen. Winsome bought the fruit pictured below. How much money did she spend on the oranges?

   a. $6.00
   b. $1.54
   c. $1.46
   d. $.50
   e. $4.50

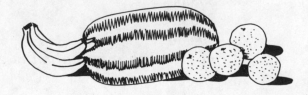

10. A roast weighing 3.15 pounds is cut into 24 slices. On the average, how much does each slice weigh?

    a. *27.15 pounds*
    b. *20.85 pounds*
    c. *75.60 pounds*
    d. *.13 pound*
    e. *1.31 pounds*

11. Barbara needed 180 inches of masking tape to mask a window for painting. How many rolls of masking tape does she need to mask 12 of these identical windows?

    a. *18 feet*
    b. *15 rolls*
    c. *192 inches*
    d. *168 inches*
    e. *not enough information is given*

12. A factory produces $\frac{7}{8}$-ton steel girders. How much steel does the factory need to produce 600 of the girders?

    a. *525 tons*
    b. *52.5 tons*
    c. *686 tons*
    d. *68.6 tons*
    e. *none of the above*

13. During the sale, Naisuon bought a 3-piece wool suit that was reduced by $47 to $95. What was the original price of the suit?

    a. *$48*
    b. *$52*
    c. *$132*
    d. *$142*
    e. *none of the above*

14. Out of 1,400 people polled, 68% were in favor of a nuclear arms freeze, 25% were against it, and the rest were undecided. How many people were undecided?

    a. *93 people*
    b. *350 people*
    c. *952 people*
    d. *98 people*
    e. *1,307 people*

15. A $1\frac{1}{4}$-pound lobster costs $7.80. How much does it cost per pound?

   a. $9.75
   b. $6.24
   c. $6.55
   d. $9.05
   e. $1.56

16. At the gas station, Verna tried to fill up her 18-gallon gas tank. When the tank was filled, the gasoline pump looked like the picture at right. How much gas was in the tank before Verna started pumping the gas?

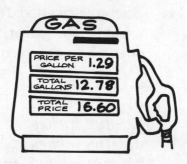

   a. .71 gallon
   b. 71 gallons
   c. 5.22 gallons
   d. 6.78 gallons
   e. 30.78 gallons

17. During the Washington's Birthday Clearance Sale, Gayle bought a $96 winter coat that was reduced by $\frac{1}{3}$. What was the sale price of the coat?

   a. $32
   b. $64
   c. $288
   d. $93
   e. none of the above

18. Shorie's rent has been increased $65 a month to $390 a month. What had she been paying?

   a. $325
   b. $455
   c. $6
   d. $600
   e. $25,350

19. Lillian's allergy pills come in the bottle pictured at right. She takes 4 tablets a day. How many tablets did she have left after taking the tablets for 30 days?

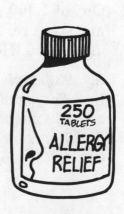

   a. 130 tablets
   b. 216 tablets
   c. 120 tablets
   d. 370 tablets
   e. not enough information is given

20. A cereal manufacturer puts 2 ounces of sugar in every box of cereal. How many pounds of sugar are needed for 1,000 boxes?

   a. *50 pounds*
   b. *20 pounds*
   c. *125 pounds*
   d. *200 pounds*
   e. *625 pounds*

21. For the survey to be considered valid, 15% of the 6,000 questionnaires had to be returned. At least how many questionnaires had to be returned?

   a. *900 questionnaires*
   b. *400 questionnaires*
   c. *40,000 questionnaires*
   d. *5,985 questionnaires*
   e. *not enough information is given*

22. An oil truck carried 9,008 gallons of oil. After making 7 deliveries averaging 364 gallons each, how much oil was left in the truck?

   a. *174 gallons*
   b. *9,379 gallons*
   c. *8,644 gallons*
   d. *6,460 gallons*
   e. *8,637 gallons*

23. In 1 week, Speculation Company's stock dropped in value $1\frac{7}{8}$ dollars to $8\frac{3}{4}$ dollars a share. What was the value of the stock at the beginning of the week?

   a. *$2\frac{4}{5}$ dollars*
   b. *$16\frac{13}{32}$ dollars*
   c. *$6\frac{7}{8}$ dollars*
   d. *$10\frac{5}{8}$ dollars*
   e. *$9\frac{5}{6}$ dollars*

24. How much would a 1.62-pound package of lamb shoulder chops cost at $2.43 a pound?

   a. *$1.50*
   b. *$4.05*
   c. *$.81*
   d. *$15.00*
   e. *$3.94*

25. Money available for financial aid at Santa Carla Community College has dropped $462,000 from last year's $1,126,200. The college decided to divide the aid evenly among 820 students who needed the money. How much did each student get in financial aid?

   a. *$563.41*
   b. *$810.00*
   c. *$1,373.41*
   d. *$1,936.82*
   e. *none of the above*

Answers on page 162.

PRE-TEST SKILL ANALYSIS		
Skill	**Item Number**	**Chapter**
Add or subtract whole numbers	13, 18	2, 3
Multiply or divide whole numbers	1, 8	5
Add or subtract fractions	2, 23	4
Multiply or divide fractions	12, 15	6
Add or subtract decimals	7, 16	4
Multiply or divide decimals	10, 24	6
Percents	4, 6, 21	9
Conversion	9, 20	7
Not enough information	11	8
Multi-step word problems	3, 5, 14, 17, 19, 22, 25	10

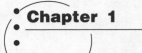

Chapter 1

Introduction to Word Problems

WHAT ARE WORD PROBLEMS?

A word problem is a sentence or group of sentences that tells a story, contains numbers, and asks the reader to find another number.

This is an example of a word problem:

Last week, Paula earned $94. The week before, she earned $88. What was the total amount of money she earned?

STEPS IN SOLVING WORD PROBLEMS

In this book, you will use 5 steps to solve word problems. It is important to follow these steps to organize your thinking. They will help you figure out what may seem to be a difficult puzzle. In all cases, read the problem carefully, more than once if necessary. Then follow these steps.

Step 1: Decide what the *question* is asking you to find.
Step 2: Then, decide what *information* is *necessary* in order to solve the problem.
Step 3: Next, decide what *arithmetic operation* to use.
Step 4: Work out the problem and find the solution. Check your arithmetic. This isn't the last step . . .
Step 5: *Reread the question* to make sure that your answer *is sensible.*

Many people can do some word problems "in their heads." This is known as *math intuition* and works well with small whole numbers. This intuition often breaks down with larger numbers, decimals, and especially fractions. Additionally, word problems of 2 or more steps can be even more difficult.

You should practice the 5-step approach even with problems that you could solve in your head. Then you will have something to fall back on when intuition is not enough.

STEP 1: THE QUESTION

After reading a word problem, the first step in solving it is to decide what is being asked for. You must find the question.

The following word problem consists of only 1 sentence. This sentence asks a question and contains the information that is needed to solve the problem.

Example 1:   How much did Mel spend on dinner when the food cost $20 and the tax was $1?

The question asks, "How much did Mel spend on dinner?"

The next word problem contains 2 sentences. One sentence asks the question, and the other sentence gives the information that is necessary to solve the problem.

Example 2:   Mary got $67 a month in food stamps for 9 months. What was the total value of the stamps?

The question asks, "What was the total value of the stamps?"

Example 3 also contains 2 sentences. Notice that *both* sentences contain information that is necessary to solve the problem.

Example 3:   The Little Sweetheart Tea Set normally costs $8.95. How much did Alice save by buying the tea set for her daughter at an after-Christmas sale for $5.49?

The question asks, "How much did Alice save?"

Sometimes the question does not have a question mark.

Example 4:   Fredi has $27 in her checking account. She wrote checks for $15 and $20. Find how much money she needs to deposit in order to cover the checks.

The question asks, "Find how much money she needs to deposit in order to cover the checks."

••••••••
Exercise 1

Underline the question in each of the following word problems.
DO NOT SOLVE!

1. Last winter, it snowed 5 inches in December, 17 inches in
   January, 13 inches in February, and 2 inches in March.
   How much snow fell during the entire winter?

2. To cook the chicken, first brown it for 10 minutes. Then
   lower the temperature and let it simmer for 20 more minutes.
   What is the total cooking time?

3. Find the cost of parking at the meter for 3 hours if it costs
   25 cents an hour to park.

4. How many years did Joe serve in prison if his sentence of
   five years was reduced by three for good behavior?

5. Jenny loves to plant flowers. She has $30 to spend on flower
   plant flats. Find the number of flats she can buy if they cost
   $1.98 each.

6. The recycling plant pays $22 a ton for recycled newspaper.
   How much did the City of Eugene receive when it delivered
   174 tons of newspaper to the recycling plant?

Answers on page 163.

STEP 2: SELECTING THE NECESSARY INFORMATION

After finding the question, the next step in solving a word problem is *selecting the necessary information*. The necessary information consists of the *numbers* and the *labels* (words or symbols) that go with the numbers. The necessary information includes *only* the numbers and labels that you need to solve the problem.

The labels make the numbers in word problems concrete. For example, the necessary information in Example 1 below is not just the number 5, but includes 5 apples. Paying close attention to labels will help you learn many of the methods shown in this book and will help you avoid common mistakes with word problems.

After each of the following examples, the necessary information is listed.

Example 1:   Doreen bought 5 apples last week and 6 apples this week. How many apples did she buy altogether?

The necessary information is 5 apples and 6 apples. Both numbers are followed by the label word apples.

Example 2:   A shirt costs $9.99. What is the cost of 5 shirts?

The necessary information is $9.99 and 5 shirts. The labels are the dollar sign ($) and the word shirts.

Example 3:   4 ounces of detergent are needed to clean a load of laundry. How many more loads of laundry can you clean if you buy the large bottle of detergent rather than the small bottle shown at right?

The necessary information is 4 ounces, 64 ounces, and 96 ounces. The numbers are followed by the label word ounces. Note that you get some of the necessary information from the pictures.

96 ounces   64 ounces

• • • • • • • •
Exercise 2

In each word problem, find the necessary information. Circle the numbers, and underline the labels. Then, on the line provided, write the label that would be a part of the answer, but DO NOT SOLVE!

1. On Friday, a commuter train took 124 commuters to work and 119 commuters home. How many commuters rode the train that day?

   _____

2. There are 14 potatoes in the bag at right. What is the average weight of each potato?

   _____

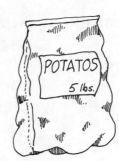

3. Unleaded gasoline costs 6 cents more per gallon than regular. Regular costs $1.47 a gallon. How much does unleaded gasoline cost?

   _____

4. To make the punch, Lona combined the bottle of ginger ale with the container of fruit juice shown at right. How much punch did she make?

   _____

5. The radio station added $38 more to the $329 already in the superjackpot. What is the new amount of money in the superjackpot?

   _____

6. Frank bought the package of loose-leaf paper shown at right and put 60 pages in his binder. How many pages were left in the package?

   _____

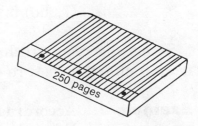

Answers on page 163.

NECESSARY VS. GIVEN INFORMATION

Sometimes a word problem contains numbers that aren't needed to answer the question. You must read problems carefully to choose only the necessary information.

Notice this important difference: The *given information* includes *all* of the numbers and labels in a word problem.

The *necessary information* includes *only* those numbers and labels needed to solve the problem.

Example 1: Nelson travels to and from work with 3 friends every day. The round-trip is 9 miles. If he works 5 days a week, how many miles does he commute in a week?

given information: 3 friends, 9 miles, 5 days
necessary information: 9 miles, 5 days

To figure out how many miles he commutes in a week, you do not need to know that Nelson travels with 3 friends.

Example 2: There are 7,000 people living in Dry Gulch. Of the 3,000 people who are registered to vote, only 1,700 people participated in the last election. How many registered voters did not vote?

given information: 7,000 people, 3,000 people, 1,700 people
necessary information: 3,000 people, 1,700 people

All of the numbers have the same label—people. However, the total number of people in the town (7,000) is not needed.

Sometimes you will have to choose necessary information from a chart or picture containing other information as well.

Example 3: According to the chart, how many hours did Eduardo work on Friday and Saturday?

given information: 4 hours, 2 hours, 6 hours, 8 hours
necessary information: 6 hours, 8 hours

In this book, you will practice choosing information from charts and pictures.

Hours Worked	
Monday	4
Wednesday	2
Friday	6
Saturday	8

• • • • • • • •
Exercise 3

This exercise will help you tell the difference between given and necessary information. Underline the given information. Circle the necessary information. DO NOT SOLVE!

1. Mona is 22 years old. She has a sister who is 20 years old and a boyfriend who is 23. How much older is Mona than her sister?

2. Rena receives $86 a month from the AFDC aid program. She also receives $67 a month in food stamps in order to help feed her 2 children. How much public assistance does she receive each month?

3. Marilyn works 3 times as many hours as her 20-year-old sister Laura. Laura works 10 hours a week. How many hours a week does Marilyn work?

4. Suzanne has a 7-year-old car. According to the chart at right, how much did she spend on gasoline during the first 2 months of the year?

Gasoline Expenses	
January	$43
February	$39
March	$40
April	$31

5. During the winter, the Right Foot Shoe Store spent $2,460 for oil heat and sold $35,800 worth of shoes. If oil costs $1.20 per gallon, how many gallons did the shoe store buy?

6. Erma, who is 45, cooks dinner for the 8 people in her family. Her husband, Jack, cooks breakfast in the mornings for only half of the family. For how many people does Jack cook?

7. In a factory of 4,700 workers, 3,900 are skilled laborers. 700 of the employees are on layoff. How many people are currently working?

8. Maritza bought the bottle of cola shown at right for $1.49. How many 12-oz. glasses can she fill from the bottle?

Chapter 2

Addition and Subtraction Word Problems: Whole Numbers

In Chapter 1, you worked on finding the question and the necessary information in a word problem. The third step in solving a word problem is _deciding which arithmetic operation to use_.

In Chapters 2, 3, and 4, you will be looking at word problems that can be solved by using either addition or subtraction. You will learn 4 methods that can be used to decide whether to add or subtract. These methods are:

> **1.** finding the key words
> **2.** restating the problem
> **3.** making drawings and diagrams
> **4.** writing number sentences

You will also work with making estimates and substitutions.

All of these methods are useful in understanding and solving word problems. After learning them, you may decide to use one or more of the methods that you find most helpful.

FINDING ADDITION KEY WORDS

How do you know that you must add to solve a word problem? Key words can be helpful. A key word is a clue that can help you decide which arithmetic to use.

Note: "How many," "how much," and "what" are general mathematics question words, but they are not key words. They help to identify the question but do not tell you whether to add, subtract, multiply, or divide.

The following examples contain addition key words.

Example 1:   What is the sum of 3 dollars and 2 dollars?

addition key words: sum, and

The sum is the answer to an addition problem. Therefore, when the word *sum* appears in a word problem, it is a clue that you should probably add to solve the problem.

Example 2:   The small cup contains 16 ounces of soda. The large size contains 6 more ounces. How many ounces are in the large cup?

addition key word: more

The word *more* suggests that you should add the 2 amounts together.

• • • • • • • •
Exercise 1

In the following exercise, circle the key words that suggest addition. DO NOT SOLVE!

1. Karen bought a new car for $5,640 plus $460 for options. How much did she spend for the car?

2. Judy bought four lemons and twelve oranges. How many pieces of fruit did she buy altogether?

3. A recipe for pumpkin pie says that an extra 2 tablespoons of sugar can be added for extra sweetness. The standard recipe is below. How many tablespoons of sugar are needed for the sweeter pie?

GRANNY'S
PUMPKIN PIE
1 tablespoon salt
4 tablespoons sugar
2 tsp. Cinnamon

4. The price of a $3 general admission ticket to the ballpark will increase $1 next year. What will be the general admission price next year?

5. Although she has lost 15 pounds, Pam wants to lose 10 more. How much weight does she want to lose altogether?

6. When Nancy did her kids' laundry, she found the coins pictured below. How much change did she find in all?

SOLVING ADDITION WORD PROBLEMS WITH KEY WORDS

You have now looked at the first 3 steps in solving a word problem:

> ● **Step 1:**   Finding the question
> ● **Step 2:**   Selecting the necessary information
> ● **Step 3:**   Deciding what arithmetic to use

The next step in solving a word problem is doing the arithmetic. People who have not learned to think carefully about word problems may rush into doing the arithmetic and become confused. However, the 3 steps before doing the arithmetic and the 1 step after provide a good way to organize your thinking to solve a problem. The actual arithmetic is only one of several necessary steps.

Look again at Example 1 from the "Finding Addition Key Words" section:

> What is the sum of 3 dollars and 2 dollars?

Step 1:   *the question:* What is the sum?
Step 2:   *necessary information:* 3 dollars, 2 dollars
Step 3:   *addition key words:* sum, and
Step 4:   *add:* 3 dollars + 2 dollars = **5 dollars**

$$\begin{array}{r} 3 \\ +2 \\ \hline 5 \end{array}$$

Now look at Example 2:

> The small cup contains 16 ounces of soda. The large size contains 6 more ounces. How many ounces are in the large cup?

Step 1:   *the question:* How many ounces are in the large cup?
Step 2:   *necessary information:* 16 ounces, 6 ounces
Step 3:   *addition key word:* more
Step 4:   *add:* 16 ounces + 6 ounces = **22 ounces**

$$\begin{array}{r} 16 \\ +6 \\ \hline 22 \end{array}$$

Once you have completed the arithmetic, there is 1 last step: reread the question and make sure that the answer is sensible.

For instance, if you had subtracted in Example 2, you would have gotten an answer of 10 ounces. Would it have made sense to say that the larger size was 10 ounces?

Exercise 2

For each problem, circle the key word or words, then do the arithmetic. Write the answer on the line below the problem. Be sure to include the label as part of your answer.

1. After 5 inches of snow fell on a base of 23 inches of snow, how many inches of snow were on the ski trail altogether?

   _____

2. According to the chart at right, what was the new bus fare in Georgetown after the 1991 fare was increased by 20 cents?

   _____

Bus Fares 1991	
Holliston	$.50
Green Borough	$.35
Georgetown	$.50
Filmore	$.60

3. What is the total weight of a 3,500-pound truck carrying a 720-pound load?

   _____

4. How big an apartment is the Dao family looking for if they want one that is 2 rooms larger than their 3-room apartment?

   _____

5. After the church raised $121,460 the first year and $89,742 the second, how much money was in its building fund?

   _____

6. According to the price chart at right, how much does it cost to buy both a sofa and a reclining chair?

   _____

Furniture	
Sofa	$529
Love seat	$319
Reclining chair	$449
Coffee table	$199

Answers on page 163.

FINDING SUBTRACTION KEY WORDS

Each of the key words in Exercises 1 and 2 helped you decide to add. Other key words may help you decide to subtract. Here is an example of a word problem using subtraction key words:

Example: The large cup contains 16 ounces of soda. The small size contains 6 ounces less than the large cup. How many ounces does the small cup contain?

Step 1: *the question:* How many ounces does the small cup contain?

Step 2: *necessary information:* 16 ounces, 6 ounces

Step 3: *subtraction key words:* less than

> **Note:** In some subtraction word problems, the key words *less* and *than* are separated by other words. This is also true for *more* and *than*.

• • • • • • • •
Exercise 3

In the following exercise, circle the key words that suggest subtraction. DO NOT SOLVE!

1. Bargain Air Lines is $25 cheaper than First Class Air. First Class charges $100 for a flight from Kansas City to St. Louis. What does Bargain Air Lines charge?

2. Out of 7,103 students, State College had 1,423 graduates last year. This year there were 1,251 graduates. What was the decrease in the number of graduates?

3. The small steak weighs 5 ounces less than the large steak. How much does the small steak weigh?

4. The large engine has 258 horsepower. The economy engine has 92 horsepower. What is the difference in the horsepower between the 2 engines?

5. This year Great Rapids has 15 schools. Next year the number of schools will be reduced by 2. How many schools does the city plan to open next year?

12 oz.

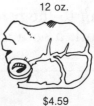

$4.59 $2.99

Answers on page 164.

SOLVING SUBTRACTION WORD PROBLEMS WITH KEY WORDS

You can now complete the example in the "Finding Subtraction Key Words" section:

Example 1: The large cup contains 16 ounces of soda. The small size contains 6 ounces less than the large cup. How many ounces does the small cup contain?

Step 1: *the question:* How many ounces does the small cup contain?

Step 2: *necessary information:* 16 ounces, 6 ounces

Step 3: *subtraction key words:* less than

Step 4: *subtract:* 16 ounces − 6 ounces = **10 ounces**

$$\begin{array}{r} 16 \\ -\ 6 \\ \hline 10 \end{array}$$

In Example 2, the key words *less* and *than* are separated.

Example 2: How much less does a $13 polyester dress cost than a $24 cotton one?

Step 1: *the question:* How much less does a $13 polyester dress cost?

Step 2: *necessary information:* $13, $24

Step 3: *subtraction key words:* less than

Step 4: *subtract:* $24 − $13 = **$11**

$$\begin{array}{r} 24 \\ -13 \\ \hline 11 \end{array}$$

This is also an example of a common type of subtraction problem. To solve it, you must reverse the order in which the numbers appear in the problem.

• • • • • • • •
Exercise 4

In each problem below, circle the key words, then do the arithmetic.

1. After a tornado destroyed 36 of the 105 homes in Carson, how many homes were left?

_____

2. How much change did Mel receive when he paid for $16 worth of gas with a $20 bill?

_____

3. After spending $325 of the $361 in her savings account for Christmas presents, how much did Carmena have left in her account?

_____

4. What is the difference in price between the 2 cars below?

_____

$12,635 $7,849

5. In the evening, the temperature had fallen 12 degrees from the afternoon high of 86 degrees, following a morning low of 58 degrees. What is the evening temperature?

_____

6. Harold weighs 161 pounds, and his wife Nora weighs 104 pounds. How much more does Harold weigh than Nora?

_____

7. Yesterday the hurricane was reported to be 420 miles offshore. Overnight it came 140 miles closer. How far from shore was it at dawn?

_____

8. Caroline's phone bill was $121 in March and $46 in April. By how much did her phone bill decrease in April?

_____

9. After the fire, Peg discovered that out of 460 books in her personal library, only 133 remained. How many of her books were lost in the fire?

_____

10. Lou bought a 21-pound sirloin strip. After the butcher trimmed the fat and cut the strip into steaks, the weight of the meat was 17 pounds. How much less was the weight of the meat after the fat was trimmed?

_____

Answers on page 164.

KEY WORD LISTS FOR ADDITION AND SUBTRACTION

Now you know that some key words may help you decide to add. Other key words may help you decide to subtract.

Here are some important key words to remember:

```
ADDITION KEY WORDS
   sum          raise
 • plus         both
 • add          combined
 • and          in all
   total        altogether
   increase     additional
   more         extra
```

You may want to add more words to this list.

```
SUBTRACTION KEY WORDS
   less than    left
   more than    remain
 • decrease     fell
 • difference   dropped
 • reduce       change
   lost
   nearer  }
   farther }   other -er comparison words
```

You may want to add more words to this list.

SOLVING ADDITION AND
SUBTRACTION PROBLEMS WITH KEY WORDS

Now that you have seen how key words are used in addition and subtraction word problems, look at the following examples to see the difference between addition word problems with key words and subtraction word problems with key words.

Example 1: It snowed 7 inches on Monday and 5 inches on Friday. What was the total amount of snow for the week?

Step 1: *the question:* What was the total amount of snow?
Step 2: *necessary information:* 7 inches, 5 inches
Step 3: *addition key words:* and, total
Step 4: *add:* 7 inches + 5 inches = **12 inches**

$$\begin{array}{r} 7 \\ +5 \\ \hline 12 \end{array}$$

Example 2: The city usually runs its entire fleet of 237 buses during the morning rush hour. On Thursday morning, 46 buses and 13 subway cars were out of service. How many buses were left to run during the Thursday morning rush hour?

Step 1: *the question:* How many buses were running Thursday morning?
Step 2: *necessary information:* 237 buses, 46 buses (13 subway cars is not necessary information.)
Step 3: *subtraction key word:* left
Step 4: *subtract:* 237 buses − 46 buses = **191 buses**

$$\begin{array}{r} 237 \\ -46 \\ \hline 191 \end{array}$$

In addition word problems, numbers are often being combined, and you are looking for the total. In subtraction word problems, numbers are being compared, and you are looking for the difference.

•••••••
Exercise 5

In this exercise, circle the key words. Decide whether to add or to subtract. Then solve the problem, and write the answer on the line below.

1. A book saleswoman sold 86 books on Monday and 53 books on Tuesday. How many books did she sell altogether?

    _____

2. After selling 15 rings on Wednesday, a jeweler sold 31 rings and 4 necklaces on Thursday. How many more rings did she sell on Thursday than on Wednesday?

    _____

3. At the town meeting, votes are recorded on the Vote Tally Board as shown at right. What was the total vote?

    _____

Vote Tally Board	
Yes	564
No	365

4. This year the Graphics Computer Company sold 253 units. Last year it sold 421 units. By how many units did sales decrease this year?

    _____

5. Mammoth Oil advertises that with its new brand of oil, a car can drive 10,000 miles between oil changes. Its other oil had to be changed every 3,000 miles. How much farther can you drive with Mammoth's new oil than with its old oil?

    _____

6. Last year, the Gonzales family paid $230 a month for rent. If their rent was increased by $35 a month, how much monthly rent are they now paying?

    _____

Answers on page 164.

Chapter 3

More Addition and Subtraction Word Problems: Whole Numbers

KEY WORDS CAN BE MISLEADING

So far you have seen one approach to solving word problems.

1. Find the key word.
2. Decide whether the key word suggests addition or subtraction.
3. Do the arithmetic the key word directs you to do.

This approach can work in many situations.

But Be Careful!

Sometimes the same key word that helped you decide to add in one word problem can appear in a problem that requires subtraction.

The next 2 examples use the *same* numbers and the *same* key words. In one problem, you must add to find the answer, while in the other, you must subtract.

Example 1: Judy bought 4 cans of pineapple and 16 cans of applesauce. What was the total number of cans that she bought?

Step 1: *question:* What was the total number of cans?

Step 2: *necessary information:* 4 cans of pineapple, 16 cans of applesauce.

Step 3: *key words:* and, total
Since you are looking for a total, you should add.

Step 4: 4 cans of pineapple + 16 cans of applesauce = **20 cans of fruit**

$$\begin{array}{r} 16 \\ +4 \\ \hline 20 \end{array}$$

Example 2: Judy bought a total of 16 cans of fruit. 4 were cans of pineapple. The rest were applesauce. How many cans of applesauce did she buy?

Step 1: *question:* How many cans of applesauce did she buy?

Step 2: *necessary information:* 4 cans of pineapple, 16 cans of fruit

Step 3: *key word:* total
Since you have been given a total and are being asked to find a part of it, you must subtract.

Step 4: 16 cans of fruit − 4 cans of pineapple = **12 cans of applesauce**

$$\begin{array}{r} 16 \\ -\ 4 \\ \hline 12 \end{array}$$

In both examples, the word *total* was used. In Example 1, the question asked you to find the total. Therefore, you had to add. But in Example 2, the total (cans of fruit) was part of the information given in the problem. The question asked you to find the number of cans of applesauce, a part of the total. To do this, you had to subtract the number of cans of pineapple from the total number of cans.

These 2 examples show that key words can be good clues, <u>but they are only a guide to understanding a word problem</u>. If you use the key words without understanding what you are reading, you may do the wrong arithmetic.

• • • • • • • •
Exercise 1

This exercise will help you to carefully examine problems containing key words. In each of the following items, the key word has been left out and the solution has been given. Two choices have been given for the missing word; circle the correct one.

1. Last week eggs cost 87 cents a dozen. This week the price _____ 9 cents. How much are eggs this week?

    87 cents + 9 cents = **96 cents**   *(fell, rose)*

2. Last week the price of eggs _____ to 87 cents a dozen. The price had originally been 78 cents. By how much did the eggs change in price?

    87 cents − 78 cents = **9 cents**   *(fell, rose)*

3. The 5% sales tax is going to _____ 1%. What will the new sales tax be?

5% + 1% = **6%**   *(increase, decrease)*

4. The 5% sales tax is going to _____ 1%. What will the new sales tax be?

5% − 1% = **4%**   *(increase, decrease)*

5. Next month, the Jones family is going to receive $14 a week _____ for food stamps. They now receive $87 a week. How much a week will they be receiving?

$87 − $14 = **$73**   *(more, less)*

6. The Johnson family's food stamp allotment has been cut. They now receive $14 a month _____, or $87 for stamps. What had been their original allotment for stamps?

$87 + $14 = **$101**   *(more, less)*

7. Gloria used to keep her thermostat at 72 degrees. To save energy, she _____ it 6 degrees. What was the new temperature in her apartment?

72 degrees − 6 degrees = **66 degrees**   *(raised, lowered)*

8. Jerline's mother came to visit for the weekend. To make sure that her mother was comfortable, she _____ the thermostat to 72 degrees. Usually, the thermostat is set at 66 degrees. By how much has Jerline changed the temperature?

72 degrees − 66 degrees = **6 degrees**   *(lowered, raised)*

9. Gail normally ate 2,400 calories a day. While on a special diet, she ate 1,100 calories _____. How many calories a day did she eat on her diet?

2,400 calories + 1,100 calories = **3,500 calories**   *(more, less)*

Answers on page 164.

RESTATING A PROBLEM

Have you ever tried to help someone else work out a word problem? Think about what you do. Often, you read the problem with the person, then discuss it or put it in your own words to help the person see what is happening. You can use this method—restating the problem—on your own as a form of "talking to yourself."

Restating a problem can be especially helpful when the word problem contains no key words. Look at the following example:

Example: Susan has already driven her car 2,700 miles since its last oil change. She still plans to drive 600 miles before changing the oil. How many miles does she plan to drive between oil changes?

Step 1: *question:* How many miles does she plan to drive between oil changes?

Step 2: *necessary information:* 2,700 miles, 600 miles

Step 3: *decide what arithmetic to use:* Restate the problem in your own words: "You are given the number of miles Susan has already driven and the number of miles more that she plans to drive. You need to add these together to find the total number of miles between oil changes."

$$\begin{array}{r} 2{,}700 \\ +\ 600 \\ \hline 3{,}300 \end{array}$$

Step 4: 2,700 miles + 600 miles = **3,300 miles** between oil changes

Step 5: It makes sense that she will drive 3,300 miles between oil changes, since you are looking for a number larger than the 2,700 miles that she has already driven.

Try this method with Exercise 2. Read the problem, then restate it to yourself. Following the problems are the types of explanations that a person might give him- or herself about whether to add or subtract. In future work with particularly confusing word problems, you should try this method of "talking to yourself" to understand the problems.

•••••••
Exercise 2

Each word problem is followed by 2 short explanations. One gives you a reason to add to find the answer. The other gives you a reason to subtract to find the answer. Put an X next to the letter of the correct explanation. DO NOT SOLVE!

1. Margi's weekly food budget has increased $12 over last year's to $57 per week. How much had she spent per week for food last year?

    ___ A.   *The budget has increased since last year. Therefore you must add the 2 numbers.*

    ___ B.   *Her food budget has increased over last year's. The new, larger budget is given. Therefore you must subtract to find last year's smaller amount.*

2. In the runoff election for mayor, Fritz Neptune got 14,662 votes, and Julio Cortez got 17,139 votes. How many votes were cast in the election?

    ___ A.   *To find the total number of votes cast, you should add the 2 numbers given.*

    ___ B.   *To find the number of votes cast, you should subtract to find the difference between the 2 numbers.*

3. The difference between first class (the most expensive fare) and the coach air fare is $68. If coach costs $112, how much does first class cost?

    ___ A.   *To find the cost of first class, you must subtract to find the difference between the 2 fares.*

    ___ B.   *First class costs more than coach. Since you are looking for the larger fare, you must add the smaller fare to the difference between the 2.*

4. It costs $36,840 to run and maintain the town's pool. During the year, $19,176 was collected from user fees for the pool, and the town government paid the rest of the cost. How much money did the town government have to pay?

    ___ A.   *To find the total cost, you must add the cost of running and maintaining the pool to the amount collected in user fees.*

    ___ B.   *You are given the total cost of running the pool and the part of the cost covered by user fees. To find the cost to the town government, you must subtract.*

5. After reading a 320-page novel, Danyel read a 205-page history book. How many pages did Danyel read?

_____ A. *Since you are looking for the total number of pages, you should add.*

_____ B. *To find the difference between the number of pages in the 2 books, you should subtract.*

6. After making 24 bowls, Claire made 16 plates. How many pieces did she make?

_____ A. *Since the number of pieces includes the number of bowls and plates, you must add them together.*

_____ B. *Since you are looking for a difference, you must subtract the number of plates from the number of bowls.*

7. A factory has produced 48,624 microwave ovens so far this year. The company expects to produce 37,716 microwave ovens during the rest of the year. What is the projected production of ovens for the year?

_____ A. *To find the projected production for the year, you must subtract the number of microwave ovens to be produced from the number of ovens that have been produced so far.*

_____ B. *To find the projected production for the entire year, you must add the number of ovens already produced to the number of ovens that are expected to be produced.*

8. Diane has a 50,000-mile warranty on her car. The car has gone 34,913 miles. As of today, how many miles will the car have left on its warranty?

_____ A. *To find the total number of miles that the car has left on warranty, you should add the number of miles she has driven to the number of miles that the warranty covers.*

_____ B. *Since Diane has driven on the warranty, you must subtract the miles she has already driven from the mileage that the warranty covers.*

Answers on page 164.

USING PICTURES AND DIAGRAMS
TO SOLVE WORD PROBLEMS

Another approach that people use to solve word problems is to get a "picture" of the problem. While some people can do this in their heads, many people find it very useful to draw a picture or diagram of the problem.

Example 1:   A recipe for 48 ounces of punch calls for 23 ounces of fruit juice and liquor. The rest is club soda. How much of the recipe is club soda?

Step 1:   *question:* How much of the recipe is club soda?

Step 2:   *necessary information:* 48 ounces of punch, 23 ounces of fruit juice and liquor

Step 3:   Draw a diagram, and decide whether to add or subtract.

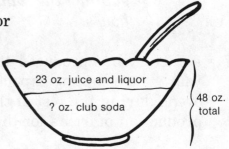

The diagram shows that you can find the remaining contents by subtraction.

punch − fruit juice and liquor = club soda

Step 4:   Do the arithmetic.

48 oz. − 23 oz. = **25 oz.**

Step 5:   Make sure that your answer is sensible.

Example 2:   After losing $237 at the blackjack table, Yolanda had $63 left for spending money for the rest of her vacation. How much spending money had she brought with her?

Step 1:   *question:* How much spending money had she brought with her?

Step 2:   *necessary information:* $237 lost, $63 left

Step 3:   Draw a diagram, and decide whether to add or subtract.

The diagram shows that you can find the total spending money by addition.

$ lost + $ left = total $ spending money

Step 4:   Do the arithmetic.

$237 + $63 = **$300**

Step 5:   Make sure that your answer is sensible.

Example 3: The oil tanker *Whyon* was loaded with 250,000
barrels of crude oil when it struck a reef and
spilled most of its oil. Within a week, the cleanup
crew had pumped all the remaining oil from the
tanker. If the cleanup crew pumped 97,416 barrels
of oil from the ship, how many barrels of oil were
spilled?

Step 1: *question:* How many barrels of oil were spilled?

Step 2: *necessary information:* 250,000 barrels of crude
oil, 97,416 barrels of crude oil

Step 3: Draw a diagram, and decide whether to add or
subtract.

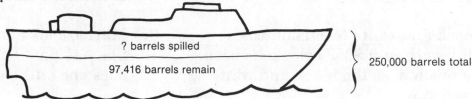

? barrels spilled

97,416 barrels remain

250,000 barrels total

The diagram shows that you can find the amount
spilled by subtraction.

total load − amount left = amount spilled

Step 4: Do the arithmetic.

$$
\begin{array}{r}
250,000 \text{ barrels} \\
-\ \ 97,416 \text{ barrels} \\
\hline
\mathbf{152,584} \textbf{ barrels}
\end{array}
$$

Step 5: Make sure that your answer is sensible.

• • • • • • • •
Exercise 3

For each problem, make a drawing or a diagram, and decide
whether to add or subtract. Then solve the problem.

1. If 3 more students are added to this
class, we will have 31 students. How
many students do we have now?

    _____

2. Rafael Hernandez paid $39 less in
taxes in 1989 than in 1990. He paid
$483 in 1989. How much did he pay
in 1990?

    _____

3. 12,000 gallons of water an hour flow through the dam spillway. The 41-year-old dam operator plans to decrease the flow by 3,500 gallons an hour. What will be the new rate of water flow?

_____

4. A $120 black-and-white television costs $359 less than a color television. How much does the color television cost?

_____

5. A black-and-white television costs $120 less than a $359 color television. How much does the black-and-white television cost?

_____

6. Between 6 P.M. and 11 P.M., the temperature decreased by 13 degrees to 61 degrees. What had the temperature been at 6 P.M.?

_____

7. At 6 P.M. the temperature was 61 degrees. Between 6 P.M. and 11 P.M., it decreased 13 degrees. What was the temperature at 11 P.M.?

_____

8. 1,412 people graduated from Lincoln High School in 1938. Today, 957 of these graduates are still living. How many of the graduates have died?

_____

9. Marion took out a loan for $6,000. She has paid back $3,800. How much does she still owe?

_____

10. A 2,600-pound truck can carry a 1,000-pound load. How much does the fully loaded truck weigh?

_____

Answers on page 164.

USING NUMBER SENTENCES
TO SOLVE WORD PROBLEMS

Addition and subtraction word problems can be solved by writing number sentences. A number sentence restates a word problem first in words and then in numbers.

Example 1: Lori went to school for 5 years in Levittown before moving to Plainview. She then went to school for 7 years in Plainview. For how many years did she go to school?

To write a number sentence, first write the information in the problem in words:

Levittown plus Plainview equals total years

Then substitute numbers and mathematical symbols for the words:

5 years + 7 years = total years

Solve:

12 years = total years

$$\begin{array}{r} 5 \\ +7 \\ \hline 12 \end{array}$$

Example 2: A play ran for 2 nights at a theater seating 270 people. 235 people saw the play the first night, and 261 people saw the play the second night. How many people saw the play during its 2-night run?

Step 1: *question:* How many people saw the play during its 2-night run?

Step 2: *necessary information:* 235 people, 261 people

Step 3: *number sentence:*

first night + second night = total people
235 people + 261 people = total people

$$\begin{array}{r} 235 \\ +261 \\ \hline 496 \end{array}$$

Step 4: **496 people = total people**

Example 3: Gloria bought a $57 dress on sale for $19. How much did she save?

Step 1: *question:* How much did she save?

Step 2: *necessary information:* $57, $19

Step 3: *number sentence:*

original price − sale price = savings
$57 − $19 = savings

$$\begin{array}{r} 57 \\ -19 \\ \hline 38 \end{array}$$

Step 4: **$38 = savings**

• • • • • • • •
Exercise 4

Underline the necessary information. Write a word sentence and a number sentence. Then solve the problem, and write the answer on the line below.

1. Ross needed a 15-cent stamp for a postcard. If he paid for the stamp with a quarter, how much change did he get?

    _____

2. Bruce drives 32 miles to work each day. When he arrived at work on Monday, he found that he had driven 51 miles that day. How many additional miles over his regular commuting distance had Bruce driven on Monday?

    _____

3. The theater company needs to sell 172 Saturday tickets to break even. How many more Saturday tickets must they sell in order to break even according to the chart at right?

    _____

Ticket Sales	
Thursday	120
Friday	145
Saturday	134

4. Wendy decided to buy a $1,300 used car. She had saved $460. She got a loan for the rest. What was the amount of the loan?

    _____

5. Becci Bachman needs 150 names on her nominating petition to run for office. She collected 119 names on her first day of campaigning. How many more names does she have to collect?

    _____

6. After losing 47 pounds, Ann weighed 119. What was her original weight?

    _____

7. Lucy's monthly food stamp allotment was reduced by $13 to $68. How much was she getting in food stamps before the reduction?

    _____

8. The refrigerator shown at right was marked down to $279. How much did Kathy save by buying the refrigerator on sale?

_____

9. John had $213 withheld for federal income tax. In fact, he only owed $185. How much of a refund will he receive?

_____

10. A car factory cut production by 3,500 cars to 8,200 cars a month. What had the monthly production been before the cutback?

_____

11. Maria earned $8,682 last year. She spent $7,991. How much did she save?

_____

12. Mr. Crockett's cow Bertha produced 1,423 gallons of milk last year. His other cow, Calico, produced 1,289 gallons. How much milk did his cows produce last year?

_____

13. Memorial Stadium has 72,070 seats. 58,682 people had seats at the football game. How many seats were empty?

_____

14. In one garden bed, a gardener grew spinach, and when the spinach was harvested, he grew green beans. The spinach was harvested after 49 days. The green beans were harvested after 56 days. For how many days were vegetables growing in the garden bed?

_____

Answers on page 165.

Chapter 4

Addition and Subtraction Word Problems: Decimals and Fractions

USING THE SUBSTITUTION METHOD

So far, you have solved addition and subtraction word problems using whole numbers. Many students can do these word problems with ease, but they worry when they see word problems using large whole numbers, fractions, or decimals.

Read the following examples, and think about their differences and similarities.

Example 1: A cardboard manufacturer makes cardboard 4 mm thick. To save money, he plans to make cardboard 3 mm thick instead. How much thinner is the new cardboard?

Step 1: *question:* How much thinner is the new cardboard?

Step 2: *necessary information:* 4 mm, 3 mm

Step 3: *decide what arithmetic to use:* You are given the thickness of each piece of cardboard. Since you must find the difference between the 2 pieces, you should subtract.

Step 4: 4 mm − 3 mm = **1 mm**

$$\begin{array}{r} 4 \\ -\,3 \\ \hline 1 \end{array}$$

Note: mm stands for millimeter. You should be able to do this type of problem even if you aren't familiar with the units of measurement.

Example 2: A cardboard manufacturer makes cardboard 6.45 mm thick. To save money, he plans to make cardboard 5.5 mm thick instead. How much thinner is the new cardboard?

Step 1: *question:* How much thinner is the new cardboard?

Step 2: *necessary information:* 6.45 mm, 5.5 mm

Step 3: *decide what arithmetic to use:* You are given the thickness of each piece of cardboard. Since you must find the difference between the 2 pieces, you should subtract.

Step 4: 6.45 mm − 5.50 mm = **.95 mm**

$$\begin{array}{r} 6.45 \\ -5.50 \\ \hline .95 \end{array}$$

Example 3: A cardboard manufacturer makes cardboard $\frac{3}{8}$ in. thick. To save money, he plans to make cardboard $\frac{1}{3}$ in. thick instead. How much thinner is the new cardboard?

Step 1: *question:* How much thinner is the new cardboard?

Step 2: *necessary information:* $\frac{3}{8}$ in., $\frac{1}{3}$ in.

Step 3: *decide what arithmetic to use:* You are given the thickness of each piece of cardboard. Since you must find the difference between the 2 pieces, you should subtract.

Step 4: $\frac{3}{8}$ in. − $\frac{1}{3}$ in. = $\frac{1}{24}$ **in.**

$$\begin{array}{r} \frac{3}{8} = \frac{9}{24} \\ -\frac{1}{3} = \frac{8}{24} \\ \hline \frac{1}{24} \end{array}$$

> **Note:** Remember, to find the solution, you must change unlike fractions to fractions with a common denominator.

What did you notice about the 3 example problems?

The wording of all 3 is exactly the same. Only the numbers and labels have been changed. All 3 problems are solved the same way, by subtracting.

Then why do Examples 2 and 3 seem harder than the first example?

The difficulty has to do with "math intuition," or the feel that a person has for numbers. You have a very clear idea of the correct answer to 4 − 3. It is more difficult to picture 7,483,251 + 29,983 or 6.45 − 5.5. And for most of us, our intuition totally breaks down for $\frac{3}{8} - \frac{1}{2}$.

Changing only the numbers in a word problem does not change what must be done to solve the problem. By substituting small whole numbers in a problem, you can understand the problem and how to solve it.

Look at the following example:

Example 4:   A floor is to be covered with a layer of $\frac{3}{4}$-in. fiberboard and $\frac{7}{16}$-in. plywood. By how much will the floor level be raised?

Fractions, especially those with different denominators, are especially hard to picture. You can make the problem easier to understand by substituting small whole numbers for the fractions. You can substitute any numbers, but try to use numbers under 10. These numbers do not have to look like the numbers they are replacing.

In Example 4, try substituting 3 for $\frac{3}{4}$ and 2 for $\frac{7}{16}$. The problem now looks like this:

> A floor is to be covered by a layer of 3-in. fiberboard and 2-in. plywood. By how much will the floor level be raised?

You can now read this problem and know that you must add.

Once you make your decision about _how_ to solve the problem, you can return the original numbers to the word problem and work out the solution. With the substituted numbers, you decided to _add_ 3 and 2. Therefore, in the original, you must _add_ $\frac{3}{4}$ and $\frac{7}{16}$.

$$\frac{3}{4} = \frac{12}{16}$$
$$+\frac{7}{16} = \frac{7}{16}$$
$$\overline{\frac{19}{16}} = 1\frac{3}{16} \text{ inches}$$

Remember: Choosing 3 and 2 was completely arbitrary. You could have used any small whole numbers.

• • • • • • • •
Exercise 1

At the end of the following set of word problems are 6 substitutions. Each of the substitutions will fit only 1 of the 6 word problems. In the answer space for each problem, write the letter of the correct substitution. (After each problem, you are told which numbers to substitute for that problem. To keep it simple, we are only using the numbers 4, 3, and 1 in the substitutions.)

1. A sweater that normally sells for $30.99 has been marked
    down by $10.99. What is the sale price of the sweater?

    Substitute $3 for $30.99 and $1 for $10.99.

    _____

2. How much heavier is the rump roast than the round roast
    shown at right?

    Substitute 3 for 3.46 and 4 for 4.17.

    _____

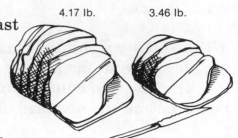

4.17 lb.   3.46 lb.

3. Robin bought a 3.28-pound steak and a 4.84-pound chicken.
    What was the weight of the meat she bought?

    Substitute 3 for 3.28 and 4 for 4.84.

    _____

4. Janice bought a dress for $31.99 and a skirt for $11.59. How
    much did she spend in all?

    Substitute $3 for $31.99 and $1 for $11.59.

    _____

5. Michael caught a $21\frac{1}{4}$-inch fish. His friend Paul caught a
    $23\frac{1}{16}$-inch fish. How much longer was Paul's fish?

    Substitute 1 for $21\frac{1}{4}$ and 3 for $23\frac{1}{16}$.

    _____

6. 2 boards were placed end to end. The first board was $40\frac{7}{8}$
    inches long. The second board was $32\frac{3}{4}$ inches long. What
    was the combined length of the 2 boards?

    Substitute 3 for $40\frac{7}{8}$ and 1 for $32\frac{3}{4}$.

    _____

A.	3 pounds + 4 pounds = 7 pounds
B.	4 pounds − 3 pounds = 1 pound
C.	$3 − $1 = $2
D.	$3 + $1 = $4
E.	3 inches + 1 inch = 4 inches
F.	3 inches − 1 inch = 2 inches

Answers on page 166.

USING APPROXIMATION TO ESTIMATE ANSWERS

When your car is in an accident and you take it to an auto body shop for repairs, you first receive an estimate for the cost of the repairs. This might not be the exact or final price, but it should be close.

When solving word problems, it is also important to have some idea of what the answer should be before you start doing the arithmetic. You can get an estimate of the answer by approximating the numbers in the problem.

An approximation is almost, but not quite, the exact number. For instance:

> In the last election, the newspaper reported that Alderman Jones received 52% of the vote and his opponent received 48%. Actually, the alderman received 52.1645% of the vote and his opponent received 47.8355%.

The newspaper did not report the exact percent of the vote; it rounded off the numbers to the nearest whole percent. Rounded-off numbers are one type of estimate.

Estimating the numbers and doing quick arithmetic in your head is a good way to check your work.

• • • • • • • •
Exercise 2

Match each word problem with one of the estimated solutions that follows. The numbers in the solutions have been rounded off. Write the letter of the correct estimated solution in the answer space.

1. During the last weekend in July, 35,142 fans saw the baseball game on Saturday. 36,994 fans saw the game on Sunday. What was the total attendance for the weekend?

_____

2. Nationwide, Grand Discount Stores sold 37,238 window fans in April and 34,982 fans in May. How many more fans were sold in April?

   _____

3. The original estimate for the cost of a nuclear power plant was .984 billion dollars. The final cost was 4.16 billion dollars. How much did the price increase from the original estimate?

   _____

4. The state budget is 3.92 billion dollars. It is expected to increase 1.2 billion dollars over the next five years. How much is the budget expected to be five years from now?

   _____

5. By expressway, it is $7\frac{1}{4}$ miles to the beach. By back roads, it is $8\frac{9}{10}$ miles. How much shorter is the trip when driving by expressway?

   _____

6. Pat is a long-distance runner. He ran $6\frac{9}{10}$ miles on Saturday and $9\frac{1}{8}$ miles on Sunday. How many miles in all did he run during the weekend?

   _____

A. 9 miles − 7 miles = 2 miles
B. 9 miles + 7 miles = 16 miles
C. 4 billion dollars − 1 billion dollars = 3 billion dollars
D. 4 billion dollars + 1 billion dollars = 5 billion dollars
E. 37,000 fans − 35,000 fans = 2,000 fans
F. 37,000 fans + 35,000 fans = 72,000 fans

Answers on page 166.

DECIMAL ADDITION AND SUBTRACTION WORD PROBLEMS: RESTATING THE PROBLEM

Restating the problem is one method that will work as well with solving decimal problems as with whole-number problems. Don't worry about the decimal points until after you have decided to add or subtract. Then, remember to line up the decimal points before doing the arithmetic.

Example: A pair of pants was on sale for $8.99. A shirt was on sale for $6.49. Alan decided to buy both. How much did he spend?

Step 1: *question:* How much did he spend?

Step 2: *necessary information:* $8.99, $6.49

Step 3: *restatement:* Since Alan is buying both items, you must add to find the total amount he spent.

Step 4: $8.99 + $6.49 = **$15.48**

Step 5: An approximation for $8.99 is $9 and for $6.49 is $6.50.

$9 + $6.50 = $15.50

Therefore, your answer should be close to $15.50. Making an approximation is a good method of checking your answer and making sure it is sensible.

$$\begin{array}{r} 8.99 \\ +6.49 \\ \hline 15.48 \end{array}$$

• • • • • • • •
Exercise 3

Circle the letter of the correct restatement, then solve the problem. Use approximation to make sure your answer is sensible.

1. Using his odometer, George discovered that one route to work was 6.3 miles long and the other was 7.1 miles. How much shorter was the first way?

   A. *Since you are given the 2 distances to work, add to find out how much shorter the first way was.*

   B. *To find how much shorter the first way was, subtract to find the difference.*

2. Max had to put gasoline in his 8-year-old car twice last week. The first time, he put in 9.4 gallons. The second time, he put in 14.7 gallons. How much gasoline did he put in his car last week?

   A.   *To find the total amount of gasoline he put in his car, you must add.*

   B.   *Since you are given the 2 amounts of gasoline, you must subtract to find the difference.*

   _____

3. The first fish fillet weighed 1.42 pounds. The second fillet weighed .98 pound. Alice decided to buy both fillets. What was the weight of the fish she bought?

   A.   *To find the total weight of the 2 fish fillets, you must add.*

   B.   *Since you are given the weight of the 2 fish fillets, you must subtract to find the difference between their weights.*

   _____

4. At the Reckless Speedway, Bobby was clocked at 198.7 mph, while Mario was clocked at 200.15 mph. How much faster did Mario drive than Bobby?

   A.   *You must add the two speeds to find how much faster Mario drove.*

   B.   *Since Mario drove faster, subtract Bobby's speed from his to find out the difference between the speeds.*

   _____

5. Last year, the unemployment rate was 7.9%. This year, it has increased to 9.1%. By how much did unemployment rise?

   A.   *To find how much unemployment rose, you must add the 2 unemployment rates.*

   B.   *To find the rise in unemployment, you must subtract last year's rate from this year's rate.*

   _____

Answers on page 166.

DECIMAL ADDITION AND SUBTRACTION WORD PROBLEMS: DRAWINGS AND DIAGRAMS

Diagrams and drawings can help you solve decimal addition or subtraction word problems.

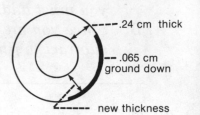

.24 cm thick
.065 cm ground down
new thickness

Example: A metal bearing was .24 cm thick. The machinist ground it down until it was .065 cm thinner. How thick was the metal bearing after it had been ground down?

Step 1: *question:* How thick was the metal bearing after it had been ground down?

Step 2: *necessary information:* .24 cm, .065 cm

Step 3: *make a drawing:* To find the size of the bearing after it was ground down, you must subtract.

Step 4: Do the arithmetic. Be sure to line up the decimal points. If you add a zero, you can see that .24 (.240) is larger than .065.

.240 cm − .065 cm = **.175 cm**

$$\begin{array}{r} .240 \\ .065 \\ \hline .175 \end{array}$$

Remember: When subtracting decimals, first line up the decimal points. Then fill any blank spaces to the right of the decimal point with zeros. This should help you borrow correctly.

• • • • • • • •
Exercise 4

Make a drawing or a diagram, then solve the problem. (Each person's drawing may be different. What is important is that the diagram makes sense to you.)

1. Meatball subs used to cost $1.60 at Mike's, but he just raised the price $.25. How much do meatball subs cost now?

   _____

2. Tara's prescription for .55 gram of antibiotic was not strong enough. Her doctor gave her a new prescription for .7 gram of antibiotic. How much stronger was the new prescription?

   _____

3. Mike Johnson was hitting .342 before he went into a batting slump. By the end of his slump, his average had dropped .083. What was his batting average at the end of his slump?

    _____

4. Joyce earned $113.50 and had $26.13 taken out for deductions. How much was her take-home pay?

    _____

5. A wooden peg is 1.6 inches wide and 3.2 inches long. It can be squeezed into an opening .05 inch smaller than the width of the peg. What is the width of the opening?

    _____

6. By midweek, Wendy had spent $46.65. At the end of the week, she had spent $23.35 more. How much did Wendy spend that week?

    _____

7. The gap of a spark plug should be .08 inch. The plug would still work if the gap were off by as much as .015 inch. What is the largest gap that would still work?

    _____

8. The King Coal Company mined 126.4 tons of coal. 18.64 tons of coal were unusable because of high sulfur content. How many tons of coal were usable?

    _____

9. Bonnie was mixing chemicals in a lab. The formula called for 1.45 milliliters of sulfuric acid, but she had 1.8 milliliters of sulfuric acid in her pipette. How much extra sulfuric acid does she have in the pipette? (A pipette is a glass tube used for measuring chemicals.)

    _____

10. Barbara complained that the 2.64-pound steak had too much excess fat. The butcher trimmed the steak and reweighed it. It now weighed 2.1 pounds. How much fat did the butcher cut off the steak?

    _____

Answers on page 166.

DECIMAL ADDITION AND SUBTRACTION WORD PROBLEMS: WRITING NUMBER SENTENCES

Number sentences can help you solve decimal addition and subtraction word problems. Look at the following examples to see how number sentences are used.

Example 1:   Meryl bought $16.27 worth of groceries and paid with a $20 bill. How much change did she receive?

Step 1:   *question:* How much change did she receive?
Step 2:   *necessary information:* $16.27, $20 bill
Step 3:   *number sentence:*

amount paid − price of groceries = change
$20.00 − $16.27 = change

$$\begin{array}{r} 20.00 \\ -16.27 \\ \hline 3.73 \end{array}$$

Step 4:   **$3.73 = change**

Example 2:   On sale, a pair of pants costs $12.49. They had been discounted $4.49 from the original price. What had the original price been?

Step 1:   *question:* What had the original price been?
Step 2:   *necessary information:* $4.49, $12.49
Step 3:   *number sentence:*

sale price + discount = original price
$12.49 + $4.49 = original price

$$\begin{array}{r} 12.49 \\ +4.49 \\ \hline 16.98 \end{array}$$

Step 4:   **$16.98 = original price**

• • • • • • • •
Exercise 5

Underline the necessary information. Write a word sentence and a number sentence. Then solve the problem.

1.   The Sticky Candy Company decided to reduce the size of their chocolate candy bar by .6 ounce to 2.4 ounces. How much did their chocolate bar weigh before the change?

_____

2. Julie's lunch cost $2.38. If she paid with a $10.00 bill, how much change did she get?

    _____

3. Bernice bought 1 chicken that weighed 3.94 pounds and 1 that weighed 4.68 pounds. She also bought a 1.32-pound steak. How much chicken did she buy?

    _____

4. The odometer at right shows Mark's car mileage when he left Boston. When he arrived in New York, the odometer read 23,391.4 miles. How long was the trip?

    _____

5. The chart at right shows the costs of subway and bus rides in Connie's city. If Connie has to take 1 bus and 1 subway to her mother's house, how much will it cost her for a 1-way trip?

    _____

Fares	
Bus	$.40
Subway	$.65

6. Judy spent $341.98 for a new washing machine in Massachusetts. If she had bought the same machine in New Hampshire, she would have paid $335.26, since that state does not have a sales tax. How much less would she have paid in New Hampshire?

    _____

7. When he ran the 200-meter race, Marcus ran the first 100 meters in 14.36 seconds and the second 100 meters in 13.9 seconds. What was his total time for the race?

    _____

8. One assembly line at the plant produced 966 soda bottles in one hour. Another line produced 50 fewer bottles than that in the same amount of time. How many bottles did the second line produce in an hour?

    _____

Answers on page 167.

FRACTION ADDITION AND SUBTRACTION WORD PROBLEMS: RESTATING THE PROBLEM

Before solving these fraction problems, you might want to use either substitution or approximation to help you decide what arithmetic to use. In this section, you will restate the problem in order to decide whether to add or subtract.

Example: Tanya grew $2\frac{3}{4}$ inches last year. If she was $42\frac{1}{2}$ inches tall a year ago, how tall is she now?

Step 1:   *question:* How tall is she now?

Step 2:   *necessary information:* $2\frac{3}{4}$ inches, $42\frac{1}{2}$ inches

Step 3:   *restatement:* Since you know Tanya's old height, and you know that she grew, you must add to find her new height.

Step 4: $2\frac{3}{4}$ inches $+ 42\frac{1}{2}$ inches = height now

$2\frac{3}{4} + 42\frac{2}{4} = 44\frac{5}{4}$ inches = **$45\frac{1}{4}$ inches now**

Remember: Whenever you add or subtract fractions, find a common denominator.

$$2\frac{3}{4} = 2\frac{3}{4}$$
$$+42\frac{1}{2} = 42\frac{2}{4}$$
$$\overline{44\frac{5}{4} = 45\frac{1}{4}}$$

• • • • • • • •

Exercise 6

Each problem is followed by 2 restatements and approximations; write either A or B on the first line to indicate which restatement is correct. Then solve the problem, and write the exact solution on the second line.

1.   A carpenter needed 1 piece of molding $28\frac{1}{2}$ inches long, and a second piece $31\frac{1}{4}$ inches long. How much molding did he need?

A.   *To find out how much molding is needed, you must subtract.*

31 inches − 29 inches = 2 inches

B.   *To find the total amount of molding needed, you must add.*

29 inches + 31 inches = 60 inches

_____

_____

2. Vera combined $1\frac{2}{3}$ cups of flour and $1\frac{1}{3}$ cups of butter in a 2-quart mixing bowl. How many cups of the mixture did Vera have?

    A. *Since Vera is combining the flour and butter, the amount of the mixture can be found by adding.*

    2 cups $+$ 1 cup $=$ 3 cups

    B. *Since you are given the amount of flour and the amount of butter, you must subtract to find the amount of the mixture.*

    2 cups $-$ 1 cup $=$ 1 cup

    _____

    _____

3. According to the scales at right, how much heavier is Tara than Erinne?

Tara

    A. *Since you are comparing 2 weights, you must subtract to find the difference.*

    71 pounds $-$ 63 pounds $=$ 8 pounds

Erinne

    B. *Since you are finding Tara's total weight, you must add the given weights.*

    71 pounds $+$ 63 pounds $=$ 134 pounds

    _____

    _____

4. Mira was $18\frac{3}{4}$ inches tall at birth. 6 months later, she was $23\frac{1}{4}$ inches tall. How much taller was Mira after 6 months than at birth?

    A. *To find how much taller Mira is, you must add the given heights.*

    19 inches $+$ 23 inches $=$ 42 inches

    B. *To find how much taller Mira is, you must subtract her birth height from her height at 6 months.*

    23 inches $-$ 19 inches $=$ 4 inches

    _____

    _____

Answers on page 167.

FRACTION ADDITION AND SUBTRACTION WORD PROBLEMS: DIAGRAMS AND PICTURES

Making diagrams and pictures can also help you solve fraction addition or subtraction word problems. To help you with your solution, use either the approximation or the substitution method.

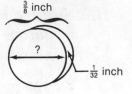

Example: Using a $\frac{3}{8}$-inch drill bit, Judy drilled a hole that was slightly too small. She used the next size drill bit, one that was $\frac{1}{32}$ inch larger, to enlarge the hole. What was the size of the new drill bit?

Step 1: *question:* What was the size of the new drill bit?

Step 2: *necessary information:* $\frac{3}{8}$ inch, $\frac{1}{32}$ inch

Step 3: *decide what arithmetic to use:* Draw a picture. Since you are looking for the next larger size, you must add.

Step 4: $\frac{3}{8}$ inch $+ \frac{1}{32}$ inch $= \frac{12}{32}$ inch $+ \frac{1}{32}$ inch $= \frac{13}{32}$ **inch**

$$\begin{array}{r} \frac{3}{8} = \frac{12}{32} \\ + \frac{1}{32} = \frac{1}{32} \\ \hline \frac{13}{32} \end{array}$$

Exercise 7

Make a drawing or diagram, then solve each of the problems below.

1. A piece of wood called a "2-by-4" (a 2-inch by 4-inch board) is really not 4 inches wide. It is actually $\frac{5}{8}$ inch narrower. What is the real width of the board?

2. Pat is at the hospital for a total of $8\frac{1}{2}$ hours a day. If during each day he has $1\frac{3}{4}$ hours for breaks, how long does he work each day?

3. Hope worked $6\frac{1}{2}$ hours and took an additional $\frac{3}{4}$ hour for lunch. What was the total amount of time that Hope spent at work and lunch?

4. A 2-by-4 is not really 2 inches thick. It is $\frac{1}{2}$ inch thinner. What is the real thickness of the board?

5. A recipe called for $2\frac{1}{2}$ cups of flour. George only had $1\frac{2}{3}$ cups. How much flour did he have to borrow from his neighbor?

Answers on page 167.

FRACTION ADDITION AND SUBTRACTION WORD PROBLEMS: USING NUMBER SENTENCES

Number sentences can also help you solve fraction addition or subtraction word problems.

Example: David planned to make a 3-inch-thick insulated roof. The roof will be made with a layer of thermal board on top of $\frac{5}{8}$-inch plywood. How thick can the thermal board be?

Step 1: *question:* How thick can the thermal board be?

Step 2: *necessary information:* 3 inches, $\frac{5}{8}$ inch

Step 3: *number sentence:*

thickness of roof − plywood = thermal board
3 inches − $\frac{5}{8}$ inch = thermal board

$$3 = 2\frac{8}{8}$$
$$-\frac{5}{8} = \frac{5}{8}$$
$$\overline{\qquad 2\frac{3}{8}}$$

Step 4: $2\frac{3}{8}$ inches = thermal board

• • • • • • • •
Exercise 8

Write a word sentence and a number sentence for each problem. Then solve the word problems.

1. Beverly filled a 3-quart punch bowl with punch. If she used $1\frac{1}{4}$ quarts of rum, how many quarts of other ingredients did she use?

2. Amy bought a skirt that was the length shown below. If she shortened it to $32\frac{3}{4}$ inches, how much did she take off?

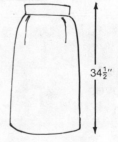

$34\frac{1}{2}''$

3. After 3 weeks in the store, a bolt of cloth that had originally been 20 yards long was $6\frac{1}{2}$ yards long. Then $3\frac{2}{3}$ more yards of the cloth were sold. How much cloth was left?

4. Last winter, Fred used $\frac{1}{8}$ cord of wood 1 week and $\frac{1}{12}$ cord of wood the next to heat his house. How much wood did he use during the 2 weeks?

5. Linda bought $62\frac{1}{2}$ inches of cloth to make drapes. She used $\frac{3}{4}$ inch for the hem. How long were the drapes?

Answers on page 168.

REVIEW: SOLVING ADDITION
AND SUBTRACTION WORD PROBLEMS

The following exercise is a review of the Chapters 1-4.

· · · · · · · ·
Exercise 9

Solve each problem, then circle the letter of the correct answer.

1. The Hammerhead Nail Company produces 55,572 nails
   and 4,186 screws a day. On Monday, 1,263 nails were no
   good. How many good nails were made on Monday?

   a. 56,835 nails
   b. 54,309 nails
   c. 59,758 nails
   d. 51,386 nails
   e. 58,495 nails

2. Ana Marie had $75.62 in her wallet. How much money did
   she have after spending $38.56?

   a. $114.18
   b. $37.06
   c. $1.98
   d. $114.06
   e. none of the above

3. The gauges at right show Ron's mileage using different
   types of gas. How much better was his mileage when he
   used gasohol?

   a. 4.13 miles
   b. 29 miles
   c. 41.3 miles per gallon
   d. 2.9 miles per gallon
   e. 1.15 miles per gallon

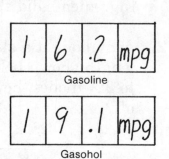

Gasoline

Gasohol

4. When Kathy bought her car, she paid $800 down and had
   $640 left in her savings account. She then paid $2,400 over
   the next 2 years to finish paying for the car. How much
   did the car cost her?

   a. $3,840
   b. $1,600
   c. $300
   d. $3,200
   e. $2,560

5. Before cooking, a hamburger weighed $\frac{1}{4}$ pound. After cooking, it weighed $\frac{3}{16}$ pound. The rest of the hamburger was fat that burned off during cooking. How much fat burned off during cooking?

   a. $\frac{4}{20}$ *pound*
   b. $\frac{1}{6}$ *pound*
   c. $\frac{1}{16}$ *pound*
   d. $\frac{7}{16}$ *pound*
   e. *none of the above*

6. Brand X contains .47 gram of pain reliever per 1.5-gram tablet. Brand Y contains .6 gram of pain reliever. How much more pain reliever does Brand Y have than Brand X?

   a. *.53 gram*
   b. *.41 gram*
   c. *.13 gram*
   d. *.27 gram*
   e. *2.57 grams*

7. A public television station has already raised $391,445 and must raise $528,555 more to stay in business. What was the target amount for the station's fund-raising drive?

   a. *$920,000*
   b. *$137,110*
   c. *$127,110*
   d. *$237,110*
   e. *none of the above*

8. Joe bought the window shade at right. When he got home, he found out that it was $2\frac{3}{8}$ inches too narrow. What size window shade does he need?

   a. *$24\frac{3}{8}$ inches*
   b. *$29\frac{1}{8}$ inches*
   c. *$28\frac{1}{2}$ inches*
   d. *24 inches*
   e. *none of the above*

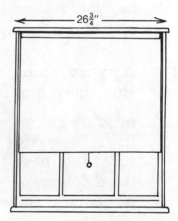

9. To heat her house last winter, Mrs. George used $\frac{5}{8}$ cord of wood in February and $\frac{1}{12}$ cord of wood in March. How much wood did she use?

   a. $\frac{3}{10}$ cord
   b. $\frac{13}{24}$ cord
   c. $\frac{1}{2}$ cord
   d. $\frac{3}{4}$ cord
   e. *none of the above*

10. A gallon of economy paint contained 3.4 tubes of pigment per gallon. The high-quality paint contained 5.15 tubes of pigment per gallon. What was the difference between the amount of pigment used for each paint?

   a. *4.81 tubes*
   b. *5.49 tubes*
   c. *8.55 tubes*
   d. *2.35 tubes*
   e. *none of the above*

11. A radioactive tracer lost $\frac{1}{2}$ of its radioactivity in an hour. Three hours later it had lost another $\frac{7}{16}$ of its radioactivity. What was the total loss in radioactivity for the entire time?

   a. $\frac{7}{32}$ *of its radioactivity*
   b. $\frac{15}{16}$ *of its radioactivity*
   c. $\frac{4}{9}$ *of its radioactivity*
   d. $\frac{1}{16}$ *of its radioactivity*
   e. *none of the above*

12. A gypsy moth grew .03 gram from the size shown at right. How much did the gypsy moth weigh after growing?

   a. *2.08 grams*
   b. *2.74 grams*
   c. *3.10 grams*
   d. *2.80 grams*
   e. *none of the above*

Gypsy Moth

2.77 grams

Answers on page 168.

Chapter 5

Multiplication and Division Word Problems: Whole Numbers

In arithmetic, there are 4 basic operations: addition, subtraction, multiplication, and division. In Chapters 2 through 4, you looked at 2 operations: addition and subtraction. In Chapters 5 through 7, you will focus on the other 2 operations: multiplication and division.

As you have seen, subtraction can be thought of as the opposite of addition. In the same way, division can be thought of as the opposite of multiplication. This concept is useful in deciding whether a problem is a multiplication or a division problem.

IDENTIFYING MULTIPLICATION KEY WORDS

In Chapter 2, you looked at addition and subtraction key words. There are also multiplication key words.

Example 1: Diane always bets $2 on a race. Last night she bet 8 times. How much money did she bet?

multiplication key word: times

Example 2: It cost Fernando $9 per day to rent a car. He rented a car for 4 days. How much did he pay to rent the car?

multiplication key word: per

Remember: Per means "for each."

Multiplication can also be considered repeated addition. Therefore, it is possible for an addition key word to also be a multiplication key word. "Total" is a word that can indicate either addition or multiplication.

• • • • • • • •
Exercise 1

In the following problems, circle the multiplication key words.
DO NOT SOLVE!

1. Miguel pays his landlord $170 rent 12 times a year. How much rent does he pay in a year?

2. During the 9 months that she stayed in her apartment, Isabelle paid $23 per month for electricity. How much did she pay for electricity during the time she stayed in her apartment?

3. At the stable, 1 horse eats 3 pounds of hay a day. What is the total amount of hay needed to feed 26 horses?

4. When her children were young, Alzette had a part-time job for 18 hours a week. She now works twice as many hours as she did then. How many hours a week does she work now?

5. Sam and Marion bought a new home on an 80-by-90-foot lot. How large, in square feet, was the lot?

6. Amy's living room is 24 feet long and 16 feet wide. What is the area of her living room?

7. Sally's research found that every dollar invested in campaign fund-raising was multiplied 8 times by new contributions. If her research is correct, how much in new contributions can she expect if she invests $3,600 in fund-raising?

8. Fresh orange juice has 14 calories per ounce. How many calories are in an 8-ounce serving of orange juice?

Answers on page 169.

SOLVING MULTIPLICATION
WORD PROBLEMS WITH KEY WORDS

Look at the following examples of multiplication key words:

Example 1: Shirley cleans the kitchen sink 3 times a week. How many times does she clean the sink in 4 weeks?

Step 1: *question:* How many times does she clean the sink?

Step 2: *necessary information:* 3 times a week, 4 weeks

Step 3: *decide what arithmetic to use:*

multiplication key word: times

$$\begin{array}{r} 3 \\ \times\ 4 \\ \hline 12 \end{array}$$

Step 4: 3 times a week $\times$ 4 weeks = **12 times**

Example 2: During the Depression, eggs cost 14 cents per dozen. How much did 5 dozen eggs cost?

Step 1: *question:* How much did 5 dozen eggs cost?

Step 2: *necessary information:* 14 cents per dozen, 5 dozen

Step 3: *decide what arithmetic to use:*

multiplication key word: per

$$\begin{array}{r} 14 \\ \times\ 5 \\ \hline 70\ cents \end{array}$$

Step 4: 14 cents per dozen $\times$ 5 = **70 cents**

Exercise 2

In the problems below, underline the necessary information, and circle the multiplication key words. Then solve the problem.

1. Artificially flavored vanilla ice cream costs 42 cents a pint. All-natural vanilla ice cream costs twice as much. How much does the all-natural ice cream cost?

2. Alan needs to buy 4 sets of guitar strings. There are 6 strings per set. How many strings will he buy?

3. Honest Furniture Company's advertisement plays on the radio five times a day and appears in twelve newspapers. How many times does its ad play on the radio in a week?

4. The We Fix-it Company charges $47 per hour to repair typewriters. The We Fix-it repairman worked for 3 hours repairing typewriters at a school. How much did the school pay for this work?

Answers on page 169.

IDENTIFYING DIVISION KEY WORDS

As you should suspect by now, there are also division key words.

Example 1: Harvey and Nancy split the cost of a $42 phone bill. How much did each of them pay?

division key word: split

> **Remember:** Any word indicating that something is cut up is a division key word.

Example 2: The nine million lottery prize will be divided evenly between the 3 winners. How much money will each winner receive?

division key words: divided evenly, each

Each is considered a division key word, since it indicates that you are given many things and are looking for one.

• • • • • • •
Exercise 3

Circle the division key words. DO NOT SOLVE!

1. Carlos, Dan, and Juan split the driving evenly when they drove from Chicago to Los Angeles. How much did each of them drive according to the map below?

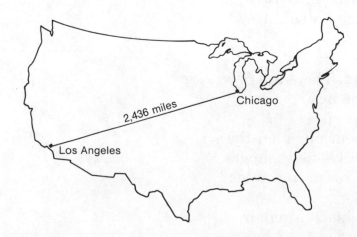

2. A bakery produced 6,300 chocolate chip cookies in a day. The cookies were packed in boxes with 36 cookies in each box. How many boxes were used that day?

3. 3 salesmen sold $2,250 worth of power tools. On the average, how much did each of them sell?

4. It cost $36 to rent the gym for the basketball game. If the 12 players shared the cost evenly, how much did each of them pay?

Answers on page 169.

SOLVING DIVISION WORD PROBLEMS WITH KEY WORDS

Knowing the division key words can help you solve division word problems.

Example 1: Union dues of $104 a year can be split up into 52 weekly payments. How much is a weekly payment?

Step 1: *question:* How much is a weekly payment?
Step 2: *necessary information:* $104 a year, 52 weekly payments
Step 3: *division key words:* split up
Step 4: $104 ÷ 52 weekly payments = **$2**

$$52\overline{)104}^{2}$$

Example 2: A 48-minute basketball game is divided into 4 equal periods. How long is each period?

Step 1: *question:* How long is each period?
Step 2: *necessary information:* 48 minutes, 4 periods
Step 3: *division key words:* divided, equal, each
Step 4: 48 minutes ÷ 4 periods = **12 minutes**

$$4\overline{)48}^{12}$$

• • • • • • • •
Exercise 4

For the problems below, underline the necessary information, and circle the division key words. Then solve the word problem.

1. The chocolate bar at right was shared equally by 4 children. How much chocolate did each child receive?

12 oz.

2. A 60-minute hockey game is divided into 3 equal periods. How long is each period?

3. A washing machine that costs $319 when new costs $156 used and can be paid for in 12 monthly payments. How much is each payment on the used washer?

4. A pack of 24 cigarettes costs 96 cents. How much does each cigarette cost?

5. Raffle tickets cost $3 each. If the prizes are worth $4,629, how many tickets must be sold for the raffle to break even?

Answers on page 169.

KEY WORD LISTS FOR MULTIPLICATION AND DIVISION

As with addition and subtraction, we can compile lists of multiplication and division key words.

> ### MULTIPLICATION KEY WORDS
>
> | | |
> |---|---|
> | multiplied | as much |
> | times | twice |
> | total | by |
> | of | area |
> | per | volume |

Generally, in multiplication word problems, you are given 1 of something and asked to find many. You can also think of these problems as multiplying together 2 parts to get a total.

> ### DIVISION KEY WORDS
>
> | | |
> |---|---|
> | divided (evenly) | average |
> | split | every |
> | each | out of |
> | cut | ratio |
> | equal pieces | shared |

Generally, in division word problems, you are given many things and asked to find one. You can also think of these problems as dividing a total by a part to get the other part.

Remember: Key words are only a clue for solving a problem. Any key word can also appear in word problems needing the opposite operation in order to be solved.

SOLVING MULTIPLICATION AND DIVISION WORD PROBLEMS WITH KEY WORDS

• • • • • • • •
Exercise 5

In the next exercise, some of the word problems have multiplication key words, and some have division key words. In each problem, circle the key words. On the first answer line, identify the circled word as a multiplication or division key word. Then solve the problem, and fill in the answer on the second answer line.

1. The pizza shown at right is to be divided evenly among 4 people. How many pieces will each person get?

_____

_____

2. An oil well made a profit of $90,000 last year. How much money will each of the 5 investors receive if all of the profits are split evenly among them?

_____

_____

3. A gas station owner charges $12 per oil change. In one day he did 15 oil changes. What was the total amount of money he received for oil changes?

_____

_____

4. In the discount store, a dress cost $27. In an expensive downtown store, the same dress cost twice as much. How much did the dress cost at the expensive store?

_____

_____

5. To earn a high school equivalency certificate, a student in Illinois must score 225 points on 5 tests but no less than 35 points on each test. What is the average score on each test that a student needs to get the certificate?

_____

_____

Answers on page 169.

DECIDING WHEN TO MULTIPLY AND WHEN TO DIVIDE

Word problems are rarely so simple that you can automatically solve them just by finding key words. You must develop your comprehension of the meaning of word problems. Key words are an aid to that understanding.

In earlier chapters, you learned that the same key word that helped you decide to add in one problem might also appear in a subtraction problem. The same is true with multiplication and division key words.

But Don't Despair!

Learning what the key words mean is the first step to understanding word problems.

In the examples that follow, you are given 2 numbers and are asked to find a third. In each example, you must decide whether to multiply or divide.

The question will ask you to find a total amount, or it will give you a total amount and ask you to find a part.

- When you are given the parts and asked to find the total, you must multiply.
- When you are given the total and a part and you are asked to find a missing part, you must divide.

To get a better idea of this and of what is meant by "part" and "total," read the 2 examples on the next page.

Example 1: Each of the city's 24 snowplows can plow 94 miles of road a day. If all snowplows are running, how many miles of road can be plowed by the city plows in 1 day?

Step 1: *question:* How many miles of road can be plowed?

Step 2: *necessary information:* 24 snowplows, 94 miles of road

Step 3: *decide what arithmetic to use:* Use the following method to draw a diagram.

Draw 2 boxes, and label them "part" and "part."

Put another box above them, and label it "total."

total

Fill in the boxes with information from the problem. Use only the information that is needed to solve the problem.

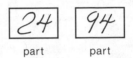
part   part

Put 24 in the first "part" box, since that is the number of snowplows. Put 94 in the other "part" box, since that is the number of miles each snowplow can plow.

The box that is empty represents the amount that you are looking for, the total number of miles of road.

Since the box representing the total is empty, you should multiply.

Step 4: snowplows × miles per snowplow = total miles
24 snowplows × 94 miles = **2,256 miles**

$$\begin{array}{r} 94 \\ \times\ 24 \\ \hline 376 \\ 188 \\ \hline 2,256 \end{array}$$

Example 2: A city has 24 snowplows to plow its 2,256 miles of road. How many miles of road must each snowplow cover in order to plow all the city's roads?

Step 1: *question:* How many miles of road must each snowplow cover?

Step 2: *necessary information:* 24 snowplows, 2,256 miles of road

Step 3: Draw and label the boxes.

total

Put 24 in the first "part" box, since that is the number of snowplows. Put 2,256 in the "total" box, since that has been given as the total number of miles.

part   part

The box that is empty represents the amount that you are looking for.

Since the total has been given, you should divide to find the missing part.

Step 4:   total miles ÷ snowplows = miles per snowplow
2,256 miles ÷ 24 snowplows = **94 miles**

$$\begin{array}{r} 94 \\ 24\overline{)2{,}256} \\ \underline{216} \\ 96 \\ \underline{96} \\ 0 \end{array}$$

Examples 1 and 2 are really discussing the same situation. In the first example, the number of plows and miles for each plow are given; you are asked to find the total number of miles that can be covered, and you must multiply. In the second example, the total number of miles are given as well as the number of plows to be used. In this case, you are looking for a missing part (the miles for each plow) and must divide.

• • • • • • •
Exercise 6

For each problem, draw "part" and "total" boxes on a sheet of paper. Then solve the problem.

1. A supermarket sold 78 cartons of Dixie cups. There were 50 cups in every carton. How many cups were sold?

   _____

2. Juanita spends an average of $6 a day for food for her family. How much did she spend during the 30-day month of June?

   _____

3. The *Washington Post*'s morning edition was 140 pages long, and the evening edition was 132 pages long. 780,000 copies of each edition were printed. How many pages of newsprint were needed to print the morning edition?

   _____

4. Fernando's car gets 18 miles per gallon. How many miles can he drive on 21 gallons of gasoline?

   _____

5. 46,720 people died in car accidents last year. What was the average number of deaths each day?

   _____

6. A factory produces 68,400 nails a day. 150 nails are packed in every box before shipping. How many boxes does the factory need in 1 day?

   _____

Answers on page 170.

USING DIAGRAMS WHEN DECIDING TO MULTIPLY OR DIVIDE

Drawing a picture or diagram is one important strategy for deciding whether to multiply or divide in order to solve a word problem. Look at how a picture or diagram could have helped you solve Example 1 from page 63.

Example 1: Each of the city's 24 snowplows can plow 94 miles of road a day. If all snowplows are running, how many miles of road can be plowed by the city plows in 1 day?

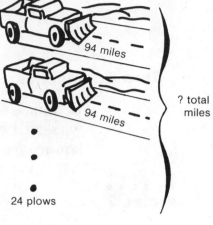

Step 1: *question:* How many miles of road can be plowed?

Step 2: *necessary information:* 24 snowplows, 94 miles of road

Step 3: Draw a diagram, and decide what arithmetic to use:

The diagram shows each of the 24 snowplows plowing 94 miles of road. To find the total miles, you must multiply.

Step 4: Do the arithmetic.

$$\begin{array}{r} 94 \\ \times\ \ 24 \\ \hline 376 \\ 188\ \ \\ \hline \textbf{2,256 total miles} \end{array}$$

Step 5: Make sure the answer is sensible.

Nearly 100 snowplows must each plow over 20 miles. An answer near 2,000 makes sense.

Example 2: A pint of floor wax covers 2,400 square feet of floor. How many pints of floor wax are needed to wax the 168,000-square-foot floor of the airline terminal?

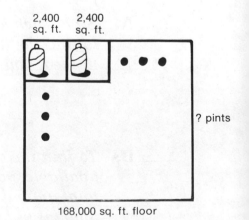

Step 1: *question:* How many pints of floor wax are needed?

Step 2: *necessary information:* 1 pint per 2,400 square feet, 168,000 square feet

Step 3: Draw a diagram, and decide what arithmetic to use:

The diagram shows that the 168,000-square-foot airline terminal floor must be divided into sections, each 2,400 square feet (the amount covered by 1 pint of floor wax). To find the number of pints of floor wax, you must divide.

Step 4:   Do the arithmetic.

$$
\begin{array}{r}
70 \text{ pints of floor wax} \\
2,400 \overline{)\ 168,000} \\
\underline{168\ 00} \\
00 \\
\underline{00}
\end{array}
$$

Step 5:   Make sure the answer is sensible.

It makes sense that the number of pints of floor wax will be much smaller than the number of square feet in the terminal.

Exercise 7

Each word problem is followed by 2 diagrams with short explanations. One choice of a diagram and explanation gives you a reason to multiply to find the answer. The other gives you a reason to divide to find the answer. Put an *X* next to the letter of the correct explanation, and solve the problem.

1.   Larry must feed each of his 380 laboratory animals 5 oz. of food pellets a day. How many ounces of food pellets does he need for 1 day?

_____ **A.**   *Since each animal eats 5 oz., to find the total ounces needed, you must multiply.*

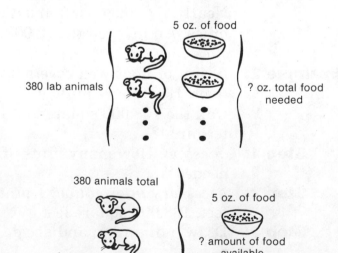

380 lab animals   5 oz. of food   ? oz. total food needed

_____ **B.**   *To find the amount of food available, you must divide the total animals (380) by the amount of food available for each.*

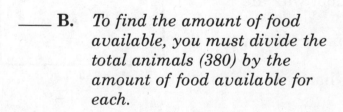

380 animals total   5 oz. of food   ? amount of food available

2. Tickets to the play were $6. At the end of the night, Janet counted $3,102 in receipts for the performance. How many people bought tickets for the play?

_____ **A.** *To find the total $ for people, multiply the cost of a ticket ($6) by the receipts ($3,102).*

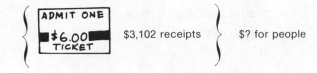

_____ **B.** *To find the number of people, divide the amount of receipts ($3,102) by the price of 1 ticket ($6).*

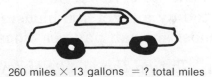

3. After filling up her gas tank, Jean drove 260 miles. After the drive, she refilled her tank with 13 gallons of gas. On the average, how many miles was she able to drive on a gallon of gas?

_____ **A.** *To find the total miles, multiply the miles for a car (260) by the gallons (13).*

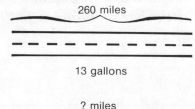

260 miles × 13 gallons = ? total miles

_____ **B.** *To find the miles per gallon, divide the miles (260) by the number of gallons (13).*

260 miles

13 gallons

? miles

1 gallon

4. Glennie planted 8 rows of tomatoes in her truck garden. If she planted 48 plants in each row, how many tomato plants did she plant?

    ____ A. *Since there are 8 rows and 48 plants in each row, you must multiply.*

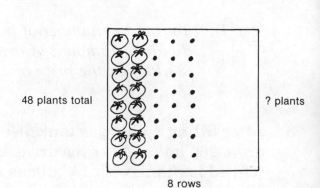

    ____ B. *To find the number of plants, divide 48 plants by 8 rows.*

5. Shirley, a buyer for a major department store, has a budget of $6,000 to buy a lot of 400 blouses. What is the most she can pay per blouse?

    ____ A. *To find the most Shirley can pay for 1 blouse, divide the total budget ($6,000) by the number of blouses (400).*

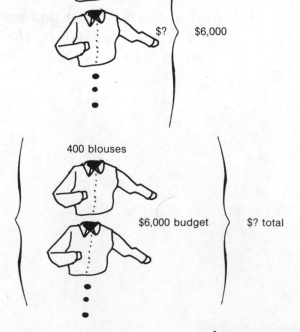

    ____ B. *To find the total paid, multiply the budget ($6,000) by the number of blouses (400).*

Answers on page 170.

• • • • • • • •
Exercise 8

Write a check (✓) next to the correct phrase by *using the solution given* after each word problem. The first one is done for you.

1. A football television contract for $78,000,000 is to be
   (___✓___ divided evenly among, _____ given to each of)
   60 colleges. How much will each college receive?

   $$\begin{array}{r} \$\ 1{,}300{,}000 \\ \hline 60 \text{ colleges })\ \$78{,}000{,}000 \end{array}$$

2. Mary bought 4 skirts for $24 (_____ total, _____ each).
   How much did she spend?

   $$\begin{array}{r} \$24 \\ \times\quad 4 \text{ skirts} \\ \hline \$96 \end{array}$$

3. There were 36,000 trees (_____ total, _____ per square
   mile) in the state forest before the fire. 48 square miles of
   forest burned. How many trees were destroyed in all?

   $$\begin{array}{r} 36{,}000 \text{ trees} \\ \times\qquad 48 \text{ square miles} \\ \hline 1{,}728{,}000 \text{ trees} \end{array}$$

4. During an average 12-hour workday, the fast-food
   restaurant sold 3,852 hamburgers. (_____ How many
   hamburgers were sold in a week? _____ On the average,
   how many hamburgers were sold per hour?)

   $$\begin{array}{r} 321 \text{ hamburgers} \\ \hline 12 \text{ hours })\ 3{,}852 \text{ hamburgers} \end{array}$$

5. A cafeteria serves 3,820 (_____ ounces of soup, _____
   people) a day, with each person being served an 8-ounce
   portion of soup. How many ounces of soup must be made in
   1 day?

   $$\begin{array}{r} 3{,}820 \\ \times\qquad 8 \text{ oz. of soup} \\ \hline 30{,}560 \text{ oz. of soup} \end{array}$$

Answers on page 170.

Chapter 6

Multiplication and Division Word Problems with Decimals and Fractions

SOLVING DECIMAL MULTIPLICATION AND DIVISION WORD PROBLEMS

Fraction and decimal word problems are solved in the same ways as word problems using whole numbers.

The following examples show a method for solving multiplication and division word problems containing decimals. As with whole-number word problems, multiply when you are looking for the total, and divide when you are looking for one of the parts. The approximation method can be very helpful with these problems.

Example 1: Gasoline costs $1.499 per gallon. How much do 18 gallons of gasoline cost?

Step 1: *question:* How much do 18 gallons of gasoline cost?

Step 2: *necessary information:* $1.499 per gallon, 18 gallons

Step 3: *diagram:*

$$\boxed{\;?\;}$$
total

$$\boxed{18}\quad\boxed{1.499}$$
part   part

$$\begin{array}{r} 1.499 \\ \times\;\;\;\; 18 \\ \hline 11992 \\ 1499\;\; \\ \hline 26.982 \end{array}$$

Step 4: price of each gallon $\times$ number of gallons = total cost
$18 \times \$1.499 = 26.982 = $ **$26.98**

(In money problems that have answers containing more than 2 decimal places, you should round off your answer to the nearest penny.)

Step 5: *approximation:* $18 \times 1.5 = 27$

This approximation shows that the answer is sensible.

Example 2: Gil's car gets 28.6 miles per gallon. Last month he drove 943.8 miles. How many gallons of gas did he need for the month?

Step 1: *question:* How many gallons of gas did he need for the month?

Step 2: *necessary information:* 28.6 miles per gallon, 943.8 miles

Step 3: *diagram:*

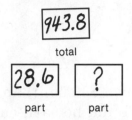

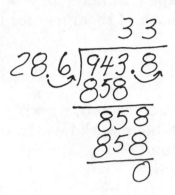

Step 4: total miles ÷ miles per gallon = gallons
943.8 miles ÷ 28.6 miles per gallon = **33 gallons**

Step 5: *approximation:* 900 ÷ 30 = 30

• • • • • • • •
Exercise 1

For each problem, use "part" and "total" boxes to help you decide whether to multiply or divide. Then solve the problem. Remember to write the labels of the answers and to round off all money problems to the nearest penny.

1. A runner ran an average of 6.5 minutes per mile for a race that had 242 official entrants. If the race was 6.2 miles long, how long did it take her to run it?

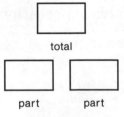

2. A nonprofit food co-op bought a 40-pound sack of onions for $11.60. How much will the co-op members pay per pound if the onions are sold at cost?

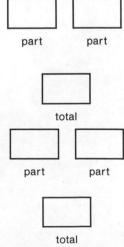

3. After filling her gas tank, Katie drove 159.75 miles. After the ride, she filled her tank again with 7.1 gallons of gas. On the average, how many miles per gallon did she get on the trip?

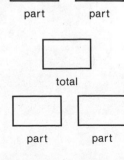

4. A beef round roast costs $2.29 per pound. How much is a 4.67-pound roast?

total

part   part

5. 4 roommates split their food bill evenly. Last month they spent $172.36 for food and $350.00 for rent. How much did each of them pay for food?

total

part   part

6. A salesman, working on commission, earned $46.56 in an 8-hour workday. On the average, how much did he earn each hour?

total

part   part

7. It cost $.85 to ride the city bus. At the end of the day, Veronique emptied the bus's cash box and deposited $167.45 in fares. How many passengers rode the bus that day?

total

part   part

8. Lynelle spent $3.65 for transportation every work day. Last year she worked 239 days. How much did she spend on transportation during work days last year?

total

part   part

Answers on page 170.

SOLVING FRACTION
MULTIPLICATION WORD PROBLEMS

When you multiply 2 whole numbers, the answer is larger than either number. But when you multiply a number by a fraction smaller than 1, the answer is smaller than the original number; for example, $21 \times \frac{2}{3} = 14$.

Multiplication and division word problems with fractions often seem confusing. When you multiply by a fraction, you may end up with a smaller number, and when you divide by a fraction, you may end up with a larger number. This is the opposite of what you have come to expect with whole numbers.

The following chart should help you remember when to expect a larger or smaller answer when multiplying or dividing.

When multiplying a number by:	Your answer will be:	Example:
a number greater than 1	larger than the number	$36 \times 2 = 72$
1	the same as the number	$36 \times 1 = 36$
a fraction less than 1	smaller than the number	$\overset{9}{36} \times \frac{3}{4_1} = 27$

(Remember, an improper fraction is greater than 1. For example,
$36 \times \frac{4}{3} = 48.)$

When dividing a number by:	Your answer will be:	Example:
a number greater than 1	smaller than the number	$36 \div 2 = {}^{18}36 \times \frac{1}{2_1} = 18$
1	the same as the number	$36 \div 1 = 36$
a fraction smaller than 1	larger than the number	$36 \div \frac{3}{4} = {}^{12}36 \times \frac{4}{3_1} = 48$

(Dividing by an improper fraction is the same as multiplying by a fraction less than 1.
For example, $36 \div \frac{4}{3} = \overset{9}{36} \times \frac{3}{4_1} = 27.)$

The most common key word in fraction multiplication problems is *of*—as in finding a "fraction of" something. Some people confuse these problems with division because they require you to find a piece of something. The example below illustrates why you multiply when you find a fraction of a quantity.

Find $\frac{1}{2}$ of 6.

You already know that this is 3. When you multiply the 2 numbers, you really multiply the numerators and divide by the denominator.

$$\tfrac{1}{2} \times 6 = \tfrac{1}{1\cancel{2}} \times \tfrac{\cancel{6}^{3}}{1} = \tfrac{3}{1} = 3$$

The following examples show you how to solve multiplication word problems that require you to find a fraction of a quantity.

Example 1:   Bernie's Service Station inspected 20 cars yesterday. $\tfrac{1}{5}$ of the cars failed the inspection. How many cars failed the inspection?

Step 1:   *question:* How many cars failed the inspection?

Step 2:   *necessary information:* 20 cars, $\tfrac{1}{5}$ of the cars

Step 3:   *key word:* of

fraction (of) × total = part

Step 4: $\tfrac{1}{5} \times 20$ cars = cars that failed

$\tfrac{1}{1\cancel{5}} \times \tfrac{\cancel{20}^{4}}{1} = $ **4 cars**

Some multiplication word problems that involve fractions do not have the key word *of*. These problems can be recognized as multiplication, since you are usually given the size of 1 item and asked to find the size of many. To go from 1 to many, you must multiply.

Example 2:   In a high school, class periods are $\tfrac{3}{4}$ hour long. How long will 8 periods last?

Step 1:   *question:* How long will 8 periods last?

Step 2:   *necessary information:* $\tfrac{3}{4}$ hour, 8 periods

Step 3:   You are given the length of 1 class period ($\tfrac{3}{4}$ hour) and are asked to find the total length of many class periods (8 periods). Therefore, you should multiply.

Step 4:   8 periods $\times \tfrac{3}{4}$ hour $= {}^{2}\cancel{8} \times \tfrac{3}{\cancel{4}_{1}} = 6 = $ **6 hours**

When you are working with a word problem and have to decide whether to multiply or divide, it is especially helpful to use Step 5: Check to see that your answer is sensible.

In Example 2, if you had mistakenly divided 8 by $\tfrac{3}{4}$, your answer would have been $10\tfrac{2}{3}$ hours. ($8 \div \tfrac{3}{4} = 8 \times \tfrac{4}{3} = 10\tfrac{2}{3}$.) Would it make sense to say that 8 periods, each consisting of less than 1 hour, would total $10\tfrac{2}{3}$ hours?

Exercise 2

In the following exercise, underline the necessary information. Then solve the problem.

Precipitation	
Baltimore	27 inches
Chicago	36 inches
New York	40 inches

1. $\frac{2}{3}$ of the precipitation in Chicago last year was rain. According to the chart, how many inches of rain fell in Chicago?

2. $\frac{7}{8}$ of the car accidents in the state last year were in urban areas. There were 23,352 car accidents in the state last year. How many accidents were in urban areas?

3. How much do 10 of the boxes shown at right weigh?

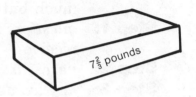

4. Brad's dog Cedar eats $\frac{2}{3}$ can of dog food and 2 dog biscuits a day. How many cans of dog food will Brad need to feed Cedar for 12 days?

5. A candy bar contains $1\frac{1}{8}$ ounces of peanuts. How many ounces of peanuts are in $3\frac{1}{2}$ candy bars?

6. Only $\frac{1}{2}$ cup of a new concentrated liquid detergent is needed to clean a full load of laundry. How much detergent is needed to clean $\frac{1}{2}$ of a load of laundry?

7. $\frac{2}{5}$ of the hamburger meat was fat. How much fat was in a $\frac{1}{4}$-pound hamburger?

8. A space shuttle was traveling 17,000 miles per hour. How far did it travel in $2\frac{1}{2}$ hours?

Answers on page 170.

SOLVING FRACTION DIVISION WORD PROBLEMS

Remember that the second number in a fraction division problem is inverted (turned upside down). Therefore, it is very important that the total amount that is being divided is always the first number that you write when solving such a problem. But even though the total amount must always come first when you are solving the fraction division problem, it does not always appear first in a word problem.

Example 1: Joyce made dinner for 9 people. She split a $\frac{1}{4}$-pound stick of butter evenly among them. How much butter did each person receive?

Step 1: *question:* How much butter did each person receive?

Step 2: *necessary information:* $\frac{1}{4}$ pound, 9 people

Step 3: *key words:* split, evenly, each

Nine people are sharing the butter. To find how much butter 1 person receives, you must divide.

Step 4: total butter ÷ number of people = butter per person

$\frac{1}{4}$ pound ÷ 9 people = $\frac{1}{4} \times \frac{1}{9} = \frac{1}{36}$ **pound per person**

Many division word problems contain the concept of cutting a total into pieces. If you are given the size of the total, you must divide to find a part—either the number of pieces or the size of each piece.

Example 2: Quality Butter Company makes butter in 60-pound batches. It then cuts each batch into $\frac{1}{4}$-pound sticks of butter. How many sticks of butter are made from each batch?

Step 1: *question:* How many sticks of butter are made from each batch?

Step 2: *necessary information:* 60-lb. batches, $\frac{1}{4}$-lb. sticks

Step 3: *key words:* cuts, each

total amount ÷ size of each piece = number of pieces

Step 4: 60-pound batches ÷ $\frac{1}{4}$-pound sticks = $\frac{60}{1} \div \frac{1}{4} = \frac{60}{1} \times \frac{4}{1} = 60 \times 4 =$ **240 sticks**

Exercise 3

Underline the necessary information in each problem below.
Then solve the problem.

1. A box is $22\frac{1}{2}$ inches deep. How many books can be packed in
   the box if each book is $\frac{5}{8}$ inch thick?

   _____

2. Gloria is serving a dinner for 13 people. She is cooking a
   $6\frac{1}{2}$-pound roast. How much meat would each person get if
   she divided the roast evenly?

   _____

3. A bookstore gift wraps books using $2\frac{1}{4}$ feet of ribbon for
   each book. How many books can the store gift wrap from a
   roll of ribbon $265\frac{1}{2}$ feet long?

   _____

4. A container contains $8\frac{1}{2}$ pounds of mashed potatoes. Linh,
   who works in a cafeteria, must divide the potatoes into
   servings the size shown at right. How many servings can
   she make from the container of potatoes?

   _____

Mashed Potatoes

$\frac{1}{2}$ pound

5. A can of Diet Delight peaches contains $9\frac{3}{4}$ ounces of
   peaches. If 1 can is used for 3 equal servings, how large
   would each serving be?

   _____

12 feet

6. Tatiana wants to divide the garden shown at right into
   $1\frac{1}{2}$-foot-wide sections. How many sections can she make?

   _____

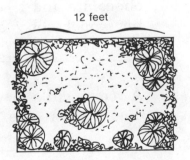

Answers on page 171.

SOLVING FRACTION MULTIPLICATION AND DIVISION WORD PROBLEMS

•••••••
Exercise 4

Underline the necessary information, and decide whether to multiply or divide. Then solve the problem.

1. A music practice room is used 12 hours a day. If each practice session is $\frac{3}{4}$ hour long, how many sessions are there in a day?

   _____

2. At full production, a car rolls off the assembly line every $\frac{2}{3}$ hour. At this rate, how long does it take to produce 30 cars?

   _____

3. At full production, a car rolls off the assembly line every $\frac{2}{3}$ hour. At this rate, how many cars are produced in 24 hours?

   _____

4. A consumer group claimed that $\frac{2}{3}$ of all microwave ovens were defective. The chart shows oven sales in one state last year. According to the consumer group's findings, how many microwave ovens sold in this state would have been defective?

   _____

Oven Sales	
Microwave	26,148
Regular	59,882

5. On a wilderness hike, 6 hikers had to share $4\frac{1}{2}$ pounds of chocolate and $1\frac{3}{4}$ pounds of dry milk. If it was cut evenly, how much chocolate did each hiker receive?

   _____

6. A recipe calls for the ingredients at right. If a cook wants to double the recipe, how much baking soda will he need?

   _____

1 tsp. Baking Powder

1$\frac{1}{2}$ tsp. Baking Soda

$\frac{1}{2}$ tsp. Salt

Answers on page 171.

REVIEW: SOLVING MULTIPLICATION AND DIVISION WORD PROBLEMS

• • • • • • • •
Exercise 5

For each problem, circle the letter of the correct answer. Round off money problems to the nearest penny and other decimal problems to the nearest hundredth.

1. 40 pounds of mayonnaise were packed in jars that weighed $\frac{1}{8}$ pound and could hold $\frac{5}{8}$ pound of mayonnaise. How many jars were needed to pack all the mayonnaise?

   a. *25 jars*
   b. *64 jars*
   c. *41 jars*
   d. *320 jars*
   e. *5 jars*

2. A 32-square-foot piece of $\frac{1}{4}$-inch-thick plywood costs $20.80. How much does it cost per square foot?

   a. *$52.80*
   b. *$11.20*
   c. *$.65*
   d. *$12.80*
   e. *$5.20*

3. To cover the cost of the prizes, a VFW post had to sell at least $\frac{1}{6}$ of the raffle tickets. They had 3,000 raffle tickets printed. How many tickets did they have to sell?

   a. *5,000 raffle tickets*
   b. *500 raffle tickets*
   c. *1,800 raffle tickets*
   d. *18,000 raffle tickets*
   e. *none of the above*

4. The trainer of the championship baseball team was voted $\frac{3}{5}$ of a winner's share. If a winner's share is $17,490 and there were 40 shares, how much money did the trainer receive?

   a. *$29,155*
   b. *$10,494*
   c. *$437.25*
   d. *$3,498*
   e. *$728.75*

5. To make 1 apron, Janice needed $\frac{2}{3}$ yard of cloth. She has a roll of cloth $7\frac{1}{3}$ yards long. If she doesn't waste any cloth, how many aprons can she make by cutting and using the entire roll of cloth?

   a. *$4\frac{8}{9}$ aprons*
   b. *4 aprons*
   c. *5 aprons*
   d. *11 aprons*
   e. *8 aprons*

6. Max used 8.1 gallons of gas when he drove 263.1 miles in 4.5 hours. What was his average speed for the trip? (Round to the nearest tenth.)

   a. *31.1 miles per hour*
   b. *58.3 miles per hour*
   c. *58.4 miles per hour*
   d. *58.5 miles per hour*
   e. *31.2 miles per hour*

7. The Motown Record Company shipped 1,410 records to the Midtown Record Store. If 30 records were packed in each box, how many boxes were needed to ship the records?

   a. *423 boxes*
   b. *470 boxes*
   c. *47 boxes*
   d. *43 boxes*
   e. *none of the above*

8. Ingrid ran in a race from Templeton to Redfield. 1 kilometer is equal to .62 mile. How many miles did she run?

   a. *24 miles*
   b. *9.30 miles*
   c. *24.19 miles*
   d. *4.13 miles*
   e. *none of the above*

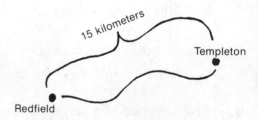

Answers on page 172.

Chapter 7

Using Proportions

Ratios and proportions can be used to make multiplication and division problems easier to solve. Proportions can also be used to work with conversions and percents (see Chapter 9).

WHAT ARE RATIOS?

A ratio is a comparison of 2 groups. Ratios can be written in a number of ways.

Example: A small luncheonette has 8 chairs for 2 tables. The ratio of chairs to tables can be written 3 ways:

8 chairs for 2 tables

8 to 2, more commonly written as *8:2*

$\dfrac{8\ chairs}{2\ tables}$

In the rest of this book, you will use only the third way of writing a ratio, the fraction form.

> **Note:** Always write labels for both the top and the bottom of the ratio.

Exercise 1

Write the following relationships as ratios in the fraction form. The first problem has been done for you.

1. 1 customer bought 6 cans of tomato soup. $\dfrac{1\ customer}{6\ cans}$

2. 2 teachers worked with 30 students.

3. Phi Hung earned 40 dollars in 8 hours.

4. Yvette drove 38 miles on 2 gallons of gasoline.

5. The company provided 3 buses for 114 commuters.

Answers on page 172.

WHAT ARE PROPORTIONS?

A proportion expresses that 2 ratios have the same value. In arithmetic, you have studied these as equivalent fractions, for example, $\frac{75}{100} = \frac{3}{4}$.

Example 1: The center of the city has 1 bus stop every 3 blocks. Therefore, the city center has 2 bus stops every 6 blocks.

$$\frac{1 \text{ bus stop}}{3 \text{ blocks}} = \frac{2 \text{ bus stops}}{6 \text{ blocks}}$$

Example 2: The ratio of women to men working at the Small Motors Repair Shop is 3 women to 4 men. If there are 8 men working at the repair shop, how many women work there?

One of the numbers of the proportion is not given: the number of women working at the repair shop. Therefore, when the proportion is written, a place holder is needed in the place where the number of women should be written. The letter n, standing for a number, is used as the place holder, but any letter could be used.

$$\frac{3 \text{ women}}{4 \text{ men}} = \frac{n \text{ women}}{8 \text{ men}}$$

Finding the number that belongs in place of the n is called solving a proportion. Look at 2 methods that can be used to solve a proportion.

Method 1:   Multiplication

Step 1: *question:* How many women work there?
Step 2: *necessary information:* 3 women, 4 men, 8 men
Step 3: Write a proportion based on the problem.

$$\frac{3 \text{ women}}{4 \text{ men}} = \frac{n \text{ women}}{8 \text{ men}}$$

$$\frac{3 \times \boxed{?}}{4 \times \boxed{2}} = \frac{n}{8}$$

Notice that both denominators have been filled in and that $4 \times 2 = 8$.

Since proportions are equivalent fractions, you multiply the top and the bottom by the same number. In this problem, the number is 2.

$$\frac{3 \times \boxed{2}}{4 \times \boxed{2}} = \frac{6}{8}$$

Step 4: Therefore, $3 \times 2 = \textbf{6 women}$.

There are cases when Method 1 does not work as simply. This is especially true when a problem contains a decimal or a fraction, or when the numbers are not simple multiples of each other. In these problems, Method 2 is quite useful.

Method 2:   Cross Multiplication

Step 1:   *question:* How many women work there?
Step 2:   *necessary information:* 3 women, 4 men, 8 men
Step 3:   Write the proportion.

$$\frac{3 \text{ women}}{4 \text{ men}} = \frac{n \text{ women}}{8 \text{ men}}$$

Step 4:   Cross multiply. Multiply the numbers that are on a diagonal.

$$\frac{3}{4} \begin{matrix} \nwarrow \\ \searrow \end{matrix} \frac{n}{8}$$
$$4 \times n = 3 \times 8$$
$$4n = 24$$
$$n = \frac{24}{4} = 6$$

> **Note:** The letter is usually written on the left side. Also, $4n$ means the same as 4 times n. It is not necessary to write the multiplication sign, $\times$.

To find n, the number of women, divide the number standing alone by the number next to the letter.

$n = $ **6 women**

Notice that when you write a proportion, the labels must be consistent. For example, if "women" is the label of the top of one side of a proportion, it must be on the top of the other side.

Examples 4 and 5 illustrate the usefulness of cross multiplication. Also, Example 4 shows the unknown, n, in the bottom of the proportion.

Example 3:   Chin has seen 6 movies in the last 9 months. At this rate, how many movies will she see in 12 months?

Step 1:   *question:* How many movies will she see in 12 months?
Step 2:   *necessary information:* 6 movies, 9 months, 12 months
Step 3:   Write the proportion.

$$\frac{12 \text{ months}}{n \text{ movies}} = \frac{9 \text{ months}}{6 \text{ movies}}$$

Step 4: Cross multiply.

Divide.

$n = \textbf{8 movies}$

$$\frac{12}{n} \diagdown \frac{9}{6}$$

$9 \times n = 12 \times 6$

$9n = 72$

$n = \frac{72}{9} = 8$

Example 4: Sandy read that she should cook a roast 20 minutes for each half pound. How large a roast could she cook in 90 minutes?

Step 1: *question:* How large a roast could she cook in 90 minutes?

Step 2: *necessary information:* one half pound, 20 minutes, 90 minutes

Step 3: Write the proportion.

$$\frac{\frac{1}{2}\text{ pound}}{20\text{ minutes}} = \frac{n\text{ pounds}}{90\text{ minutes}}$$

$$\frac{\frac{1}{2}}{20} \diagdown \frac{n}{90}$$

$20 \times n = 90 \times \frac{1}{2}$

$20n = 45$

$n = \frac{45}{20} = 2\frac{1}{4}$

Step 4: Cross multiply.

Divide.

$n = \textbf{2}\frac{1}{4}\textbf{ pounds of roast}$

• • • • • • • •

Exercise 2

Solve the following proportions for n.

1. $\dfrac{160\text{ miles}}{5\text{ hours}} = \dfrac{n\text{ miles}}{10\text{ hours}}$

    _____

6. $\dfrac{\$4.39}{1\text{ shirt}} = \dfrac{n\text{ dollars}}{6\text{ shirts}}$

    _____

2. $\dfrac{12\text{ cars}}{32\text{ people}} = \dfrac{3\text{ cars}}{n\text{ people}}$

    _____

7. $\dfrac{\$17.85}{3\text{ shirts}} = \dfrac{n\text{ dollars}}{10\text{ shirts}}$

    _____

3. $\dfrac{n\text{ dollars}}{8\text{ quarters}} = \dfrac{6\text{ dollars}}{24\text{ quarters}}$

    _____

8. $\dfrac{3\text{ minutes}}{\frac{1}{2}\text{ mile}} = \dfrac{n\text{ minutes}}{5\text{ miles}}$

    _____

4. $\dfrac{42\text{ pounds}}{n\text{ chickens}} = \dfrac{14\text{ pounds}}{4\text{ chickens}}$

    _____

9. $\dfrac{575\text{ passengers}}{n\text{ days}} = \dfrac{1,725\text{ passengers}}{21\text{ days}}$

    _____

5. $\dfrac{28,928\text{ people}}{8\text{ doctors}} = \dfrac{n\text{ people}}{1\text{ doctor}}$

    _____

10. $\dfrac{7\text{ blinks}}{\frac{1}{10}\text{ minute}} = \dfrac{n\text{ blinks}}{10\text{ minutes}}$

    _____

Answers on page 172.

USING PROPORTIONS TO SOLVE
MULTIPLICATION AND DIVISION WORD PROBLEMS

Proportions can be used when you are unsure of whether to multiply or divide.

The following examples show how to write proportions to solve multiplication and division word problems.

Example 1: There are 16 cups in a gallon. At the church picnic, Carmella poured 5 gallons of Coke into paper cups that each held 1 cup of soda. How many cups did she fill?

Step 1: *question:* How many cups did she fill?

Step 2: *necessary information:* 16 cups in a gallon, 5 gallons, 1 cup

Step 3: Write the proportion.

labels for proportion: $\dfrac{\text{cups}}{\text{gallons}}$

$$\frac{16 \text{ cups}}{1 \text{ gallon}} = \frac{n \text{ cups}}{5 \text{ gallons}}$$

Step 4: Cross multiply.

(*n* means the same as $1 \times n$. From now on you don't need to write the 1 and the $\times$ sign, so you write $n = 16 \times 5$.)

$n = \textbf{80 cups}$

Remember: When you write the labels for a proportion, it doesn't matter which category goes on top. But once you make a decision, you must stick with it. Once you put "cups" on the top of one ratio, you must keep "cups" on top of the other.

16 cups in a gallon means the same as $\dfrac{16 \text{ cups}}{1 \text{ gallon}}$. The 1 will often not appear in these word problems. When writing a proportion, you must determine when a 1 is needed and where it goes. You can do this by first identifying the 2 labels and then putting numbers in the proportion.

There are a number of word phrases that require that a 1 be used in a ratio. Some examples are:

Phrases	Meaning
27 miles per gallon	$\dfrac{27 \text{ miles}}{1 \text{ gallon}}$
$8 an hour	$\dfrac{\$8}{1 \text{ hour}}$
3 meals a day	$\dfrac{3 \text{ meals}}{1 \text{ day}}$
30 miles each day	$\dfrac{30 \text{ miles}}{1 \text{ day}}$

Example 2: At the Boardwalk Arcade, owner Manuel Santos collects 1,380 quarters every day. There are 4 quarters in a dollar. How many dollars does he collect every day?

Step 1: *question:* How many dollars does he collect every day?

Step 2: *necessary information:* 1,380 quarters, 4 quarters in a dollar

Step 3: *labels for proportion:* $\dfrac{\text{dollars}}{\text{quarters}}$

$$\frac{n \text{ dollars}}{1,380 \text{ quarters}} = \frac{1 \text{ dollar}}{4 \text{ quarters}}$$

Step 4: Cross multiply.

Divide.

$n = \mathbf{345}$ **dollars**

$$\frac{n}{1,380} \diagup \frac{1}{4}$$

$$4 \times n = 1,380 \times 1$$
$$4n = 1,380$$

$$n = \frac{1,380}{4} = 345$$

• • • • • • • •
Exercise 3

Underline the necessary information. Write proportions for the problems below, then solve them.

1. A shipment of vaccine can protect 7,800 people. How many shipments of vaccine are needed to protect 140,400 people living in the Portland area?

    _____

2. It costs $340 an hour to run the 1,000-watt power generator. How much does it cost to run the generator for 24 hours?

_____

3. How many ounces of soup (like the can shown at right) are in a carton containing 28 cans?

_____

4. Jim types 52 words per minute. How many words did he type when he typed for 26 minutes?

_____

5. An elementary school nurse used 3,960 Band-Aids last year. There were 180 school days. On the average, how many Band-Aids did he use a day?

_____

6. The company health clinic gave out 5,460 aspirin and 720 antacid tablets last year. How many bottles of aspirin did the clinic use last year if there were 260 aspirin in a bottle?

_____

7. A coal mine produced 126 tons of slag in a week. Trucks removed the slag in 3-ton loads. How many loads were needed to remove all the slag?

_____

8. Cloth is sold by the yard. Edyth bought the piece of cloth shown at right to make dresses. There are 3 feet in a yard. How many yards of cloth did she buy?

_____

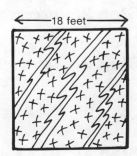

9. A 6-ounce can of water chestnuts contains 26 water chestnuts. Hong used 3 cans of water chestnuts. How many water chestnuts did she use?

_____

Answers on page 173.

USING PROPORTIONS TO SOLVE DECIMAL MULTIPLICATION AND DIVISION WORD PROBLEMS

You can use proportions to solve decimal multiplication and division word problems. The problems should be set up as if the numbers were whole numbers. Multiply or divide as if you were using whole numbers. Then use the rules for decimal multiplication and division to place the decimal point in the right place. Finally, round off the answer if necessary.

Example 1: Ray has $15.00 to spend on gasoline. How many gallons can he buy if 1 gallon costs $1.20?

Step 1: *question:* How many gallons can he buy?

Step 2: *necessary information:* $15.00, $1.20

Step 3: *labels for proportion:* $\dfrac{\$}{\text{gallons}}$

$$\frac{\$15.00}{n \text{ gallons}} = \frac{\$1.20}{1 \text{ gallon}}$$

Step 4: Cross multiply.

Divide.

$n = \textbf{12.5 gallons}$

$$\frac{15}{n} = \frac{1.20}{1}$$

$1.20 \times n = 15 \times 1$
$1.20n = 15$

$$n = \frac{15}{1.20} = 12.5$$

Example 2: There are 236.5 milliliters in a cup. A recipe calls for 3 cups of flour. Maria has only metric spoons and measuring cups. How many milliliters of flour does she need for the recipe?

Step 1: *question:* How many milliliters of flour does she need for the recipe?

Step 2: *necessary information:* 236.5 milliliters in a cup, 3 cups

Step 3: *labels for proportion:* $\dfrac{\text{milliliters}}{\text{cups}}$

$$\frac{236.5 \text{ milliliters}}{1 \text{ cup}} = \frac{n \text{ milliliters}}{3 \text{ cups}}$$

Step 4: Cross multiply.

$n = \textbf{709.5 milliliters}$

$$\frac{236.5}{1} = \frac{n}{3}$$

$n = 3 \times 236.5$
$n = 709.5$

• • • • • • •
Exercise 4

Underline the necessary information. Write the labels for the proportion, fill in the numbers, then solve the proportion. Round your answers to the nearest hundredth.

1. There are 25.4 millimeters in an inch. How many inches long is a 100-millimeter cigarette?

   _____

2. A kilogram weight is shown at right. The police seized 36 kilograms of illegal drugs. How many pounds did the drugs weigh?

   _____

3. Alba worked 35.5 hours last week. She earns $4.62 an hour. How much money did she earn last week?

   _____

4. There are 1.09 yards in a meter. Gary ran in an 880-yard race. How many meters did he run?

   _____

5. Cindy spent $20.00 on gasoline. The gasoline cost $1.15 per gallon. How many gallons of gasoline did she buy?

   _____

6. There are approximately 1.61 kilometers in a mile. The speedometer on Iris's imported car is in kilometers per hour. She does not want to speed. What is 55 miles per hour in kilometers per hour?

   _____

7. A Tiger Milk Nutrition Bar weighs 35.4 grams. The factory processed 9,486 bars in one run. How many grams of Tiger Milk bars were processed?

   _____

Answers on page 174.

USING PROPORTIONS TO SOLVE FRACTION MULTIPLICATION AND DIVISION WORD PROBLEMS

Proportions can be used to solve multiplication and division word problems containing fractions. Though they look complicated when you set them up, they are manageable after you cross multiply.

Example 1: A dump truck can carry a load of $2\frac{3}{4}$ tons of gravel. In one day, the truck removed 8 loads of gravel from a gravel pit. How many tons of gravel did it remove from the pit that day?

  Step 1: *question:* How many tons of gravel did it remove from the pit that day?

  Step 2: *necessary information:* a load of $2\frac{3}{4}$ tons, 8 loads

  Step 3: *labels for proportion:* $\dfrac{\text{tons}}{\text{loads}}$

  $$\frac{2\frac{3}{4}\ \text{tons}}{1\ \text{load}} = \frac{n\ \text{tons}}{8\ \text{loads}}$$

  Step 4: Cross multiply.

  $n = \textbf{22 tons}$

$$\frac{2\frac{3}{4}}{1} \diagdown\!\!\!\!\diagup \frac{n}{8}$$

$$n = 8 \times 2\frac{3}{4}$$

$$n = \overset{2}{8} \times \frac{11}{\cancel{4}_1} = 22$$

Example 2: Burger King makes a $\frac{1}{4}$-pound hamburger. How many of these hamburgers can be made from 50 pounds of hamburger meat?

  Step 1: *question:* How many of these hamburgers can be made?

  Step 2: *necessary information:* $\frac{1}{4}$ pound, 50 pounds

  Step 3: *labels for proportion:* $\dfrac{\text{pounds}}{\text{hamburgers}}$

  $$\frac{\frac{1}{4}\ \text{pound}}{1\ \text{hamburger}} = \frac{50\ \text{pounds}}{n\ \text{hamburgers}}$$

  Step 4: Cross multiply.

  $n = \textbf{200 hamburgers}$

$$\frac{\frac{1}{4}}{1} \diagdown\!\!\!\!\diagup \frac{50}{n}$$

$$\frac{1}{4} \times n = 50 \times 1$$

$$\frac{1}{4}n = 50$$

$$n = 50 \times 4 = 200$$

A word problem asking you to find a fraction of something is easier to solve by direct multiplication than by using a proportion. Example 3 illustrates this.

Example 3: $\frac{2}{5}$ of all gallons of milk sold in a store are low-fat. The store sold 380 gallons of milk. How many gallons of low-fat milk were sold?

You could set up the following proportion to solve the problem:

$$\frac{\frac{2}{5} \text{ low-fat}}{1 \text{ gallon}} = \frac{n \text{ low-fat}}{380 \text{ gallons}}$$

While this will give you the correct answer, it is easier to remember that you should multiply to find a fraction of something. It is easier to solve the problem this way:

fraction (of) × total gallons = low-fat gallons

$$\frac{2}{\underset{1}{\cancel{5}}} \times \frac{\cancel{380}^{76}}{1} = \frac{2}{1} \times \frac{76}{1} = \textbf{152 gallons}$$

• • • • • • • •
Exercise 5

Underline the necessary information in each problem below. Write the proportions, and solve the problems.

1. A slicing machine cut roast beef $\frac{1}{16}$ inch thick. The giant sandwich was advertised to contain roast beef 2 inches thick. How many slices of roast beef were on the sandwich?

   _____

2. The La Ronga Bakery baked 1,460 loaves of bread in 1 day. If each loaf contained $1\frac{3}{4}$ teaspoons of salt, how much salt did the bakery use?

   _____

3. How many books $\frac{7}{8}$ inch thick can be packed in a box 35 inches deep?

   _____

4. A can of pears weighs $9\frac{2}{3}$ ounces. There are 16 cans of pears in a carton. How many ounces does a carton of pears weigh?

   _____

5. There are 8 cups of detergent in a bottle of Easy Clean Detergent. $\frac{1}{4}$ cup is all that is needed for 1 load of laundry. How many loads of laundry can be cleaned with a bottle of Easy Clean?

   _____

Answers on page 174.

SOLVING CONVERSION WORD PROBLEMS

Have you ever seen this kind of problem?

Example 1:   Caren has a 204-inch roll of masking tape. How many feet of molding can she cover with the roll?

This problem is an example of a type of multiplication or division word problem that contains only 1 number and requires outside information in order to be solved. These are word problems involving conversions from one type of measurement to another.

Here is the solution and explanation of the example:

Step 1:   *question:* How many feet?
Step 2:   *necessary information:* 204 inches

Notice that the question asks for a solution that has a different label than what is given in the problem. To solve this, you must know how to convert inches to feet. Then you can set up a proportion to solve the problem.

Step 3:   12 inches = 1 foot

$$\text{labels for proportion:} \frac{\text{inches}}{\text{feet}}$$

The conversion will be one side of the proportion.

$$\frac{12 \text{ inches}}{1 \text{ foot}} = \frac{204 \text{ inches}}{n \text{ feet}}$$

Step 4:   Cross multiply.

Divide.

$n = \textbf{17 feet}$

$$\frac{12}{1} \diagup \frac{204}{n}$$

$12 \times n = 204 \times 1$
$12n = 204$
$n = \dfrac{204}{12} = 17$

A diagram can often help you picture a conversion word problem.

Example 2: The Spring Lake Day-Care Center gives each of its 12 children a cup of milk for lunch every day. How many quarts of milk does the Center use each day?

Step 1: *question:* How many quarts of milk does the center use each day?

Step 2: *necessary information:* 12 cups, 1 cup

conversion formula: 4 cups = 1 quart

Step 3: Decide what arithmetic to use.

The diagram shows that you should divide:

number of cups ÷ cups in a quart = number of quarts

Step 4: Do the arithmetic:

$$12 \text{ cups} \div \frac{4 \text{ cups}}{1 \text{ quart}} = \textbf{3 quarts}$$

Step 5: Make sure the answer is sensible. Look at the diagram to see that the answer of 3 quarts makes sense.

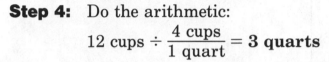

Exercise 6

Use the conversion chart on the next page to help you write the conversion and the proportion for each problem. Then solve the problem.

1. How many years old was Gloria's 30-month-old daughter?

2. A 200-gallon batch of ketchup was bottled in quart bottles. How many bottles were filled?

3. How many kilometers long is a 10,000-meter road race?

4. Paul's truck can carry a ½-ton load. How many pounds of gravel can it carry?

5. José brought the cream shown at right to the outing. How many ounces of cream did he bring?

6. Mt. Everest is 29,028 feet high. How many miles high is Mt. Everest? (Round off to the nearest tenth.)

Answers on page 175.

Many word problems cannot be solved unless you know a conversion. Here are lists of some common measurements and their conversions.

Time Conversions
365 days = 1 year
12 months = 1 year
52 weeks = 1 year
7 days = 1 week
24 hours = 1 day
60 minutes = 1 hour
60 seconds = 1 minute

Length and Area Conversions
5,280 feet = 1 mile
1,760 yards = 1 mile
3 feet = 1 yard
36 inches = 1 yard
12 inches = 1 foot
144 square inches = 1 square foot
1,000 meters = 1 kilometer
100 centimeters = 1 meter
1,000 millimeters = 1 meter
10 millimeters = 1 centimeter

Weight Conversions
2,000 pounds = 1 ton
16 ounces = 1 pound
1,000 grams = 1 kilogram
1,000 milligrams = 1 gram

Volume Conversions
4 quarts = 1 gallon
2 pints = 1 quart
4 cups = 1 quart
2 cups = 1 pint
32 ounces = 1 quart
16 ounces = 1 pint
8 ounces = 1 cup
1,000 milliliters = 1 liter

USING PROPORTIONS TO SOLVE WORD PROBLEMS CONTAINING BOTH A FRACTION AND A DECIMAL

Sometimes you will find a multiplication or division word problem in which one number is a decimal and the other is a fraction. The proportion method is very useful in solving this type of word problem.

Example: A $\frac{3}{4}$-pound steak cost $6.75. How much did it cost per pound?

Step 1: *question:* How much did it cost per pound?

Step 2: *necessary information:* $\frac{3}{4}$ pound, $6.75

Step 3: *labels for proportion:* pound, $

$$\frac{\frac{3}{4} \text{ pound}}{\$6.75} = \frac{1 \text{ pound}}{\$n}$$

Step 4: Cross multiply.

Divide.

$n = \mathbf{\$9.00}$

$$\frac{\frac{3}{4}}{6.75} \diagup^{1}_{n}$$

$$\frac{3}{4}n = 6.75$$

$$n = \overset{2.25}{\cancel{6.75}} \times \frac{4}{\cancel{3}}$$

$$n = 9.00$$

If you had not been able to cancel in the example, you would have multiplied the numerators (tops) and divided by the product of the denominators (bottoms). Be careful to keep the decimal point in the correct place.

●●●●●●●
Exercise 7

Write the proportions and solve the problems below. (Round off money problems to the nearest penny.)

1. Cloth was being sold at $12.60 a yard. Lori bought $3\frac{1}{3}$ yards of cloth. How much did she spend?

2. 13.5 pounds of time-release fertilizer is supposed to last $4\frac{1}{2}$ years. How much fertilizer is used up each year?

3. Murray bought $2\frac{2}{3}$ pounds of grapes for $3.25. How much did the grapes cost per pound?

4. Marty took pictures at graduation. He used $7\frac{1}{2}$ rolls of film, and was charged $384.50. What was the charge per roll of film?

Answers on page 175.

USING PROPORTIONS TO SOLVE MULTIPLICATION AND DIVISION WORD PROBLEMS

• • • • • • • •
Exercise 8

Underline the necessary information. Write the proportions, then solve the problems.

1. A butcher can cut up a chicken in $\frac{1}{12}$ of an hour. How many chickens can he cut up in an 8-hour work day?

2. A nurse can take 8 blood samples in 60 minutes. How long does it take her to take 1 blood sample?

3. A mile is about 1.6 kilometers. How many kilometers is a 26-mile marathon?

4. An oil-drilling rig can drill 6 feet in an hour. How far can it drill in 24 hours?

5. A gram is .04 ounce. How many grams are in a 12-ounce can of pineapple juice?

6. Rose uses $3\frac{1}{4}$ pounds of pumpkin to make 2 pumpkin pies. For a fall bake sale, she made 10 pies. How many pounds of pumpkin did she use?

7. When the floodgates were opened, 68,000 gallons of water flowed over the dam per hour. How many gallons flowed over the dam in a day?

8. Lace trimming costs $.12 per foot. How much did Zelda spend on $4\frac{1}{4}$ feet of trimming?

9. Superglue sets in $3\frac{1}{2}$ minutes. In how many seconds does Superglue set?

10. A 942-page book contained 302,382 words. On the average, how many words were on each page?

Answers on page 175.

Chapter 8

Strategies with Mixed Word Problems

So far, you have worked with word problems that have been divided into two major categories—addition/subtraction problems and multiplication/division problems.

In most situations, you will be faced with the 4 types of problems mixed together. Always read each problem carefully to get an understanding of the situation it describes. This will help you choose the right arithmetic.

Keep these general guidelines in mind:

- when combining amounts ────────► add
- when finding the difference between 2 amounts ────────► subtract
- when given 1 unit of something and asked to find several ────────► multiply
- when asked to find a fraction of a quantity ────────► multiply
- when given the amount for several and asked for 1 ────────► divide
- when splitting, cutting, sharing, etc. ─► divide

Working through the following exercises will help sharpen your skills with word problems when the different types are mixed together.

MIXED WORD PROBLEMS WITH WHOLE NUMBERS

Exercise 1

On the line below each problem, write the arithmetic operation that you would use to solve it: addition, subtraction, multiplication, or division. DO NOT SOLVE!

1. Doreen needs 39 credits to complete her bachelor's degree at the state university. The university charges $165 per credit for tuition. How much will Doreen have to pay in tuition if she completes her degree?

   _____

2. Alan wrote a 74,200-word manuscript for his new book. The typesetter estimates that there will be an average of 280 words per page. If the typesetter is correct, how many pages will there be in the book?

    _____

3. After laying off 27 workers, Paul still had 168 workers at the hospital. How many workers were there at the hospital before the changes?

    _____

4. A department store bought shirts for $4 each and sold them for $8. How much profit did it make on each shirt?

    _____

5. Tom needs 19 feet of molding for each doorway in his home. The home will have 9 doorways. How much molding does he need?

    _____

6. Part of Rob's harvesting log is shown at right. How many more ears of corn did he harvest on Thursday than on Wednesday?

    _____

	WED	THURS
Corn	476	548
Zucchini	94	129

7. As coach of her soccer team, Althea decided that all 22 players would get equal playing time. With a total of 990 minutes to distribute, how many playing minutes did Althea give to each of her players?

    _____

8. At her day-care center, Beth used an entire gallon of juice at snack time for 24 children. On the average, how many ounces of juice did each child receive?

    _____

9. The governor's goal is to reduce the state's imports of foreign oil by 25,000 barrels to 90,000 barrels a month. How much oil is the state currently importing a month?

    _____

Answers on page 176.

USING LABELS TO SOLVE WORD PROBLEMS

Every number in a word problem has a label. Every number *refers* to something. In other words, it makes no sense to say simply "7" or "$38\frac{1}{2}$." We need to know—7 *what*? $38\frac{1}{2}$ *what*? Dogs? Miles per hour? Years old? What do these numbers refer to?

Paying careful attention to labels will help you decide whether to add, subtract, multiply, or divide. Look at the following example:

Example 1:   On Saturday night, Bruce spent $46.50 on dinner and $38.00 for tickets to a play. How much did he spend altogether?

Notice that the labels of both pieces of the necessary information are *dollars*. Also, you can tell that the label of the answer will be in *dollars*. You probably already have figured out that you need to add $46.50 and $38.00 to solve the problem.

Look at the next example:

Example 2:   35,102 women and 29,952 men voted in the last election. How many people voted?

The labels of the necessary information and the answer are different. Does this mean you should not add or subtract?

Whenever the labels of items in a word problem are different, first ask yourself if the different labels can be part of a *broader category* or if they can be *converted* to a common unit (such as from *pounds* to *ounces* or from *years* to *months*). For example, men and women can both be considered part of the broader category of *people*; therefore, all the labels in the problem are the same and you can add or subtract to find the answer. For the problem above, you should add 35,102 and 29,952 to get the answer.

Using labels to decide whether to multiply or to divide is a bit trickier. However, if you are willing to "play" a bit with the labels in a problem, you can often make this decision before you have to work with actual numbers. Read the next example:

> You will often find this pattern in word problems:
>
> WHEN THE LABELS OF ALL THE NECESSARY INFORMATION AND THE ANSWER ARE THE SAME, YOU NEED TO *ADD OR SUBTRACT* TO SOLVE.

Example 3:   Ken drove 385 miles in 7 hours. How many miles per hour did he average on this trip?

The labels of one piece of the necessary information is *miles*; the label of the other piece is *hours*. The label of the answer is *miles per hour*. Already you may be guessing that you should not add or subtract, for the labels are *not* the same and they can't be converted to a common unit.

The answer will be in *miles per hour*, which can also be written as $\frac{miles}{hour}$ (miles *divided by* 1 hour). Set up a statement using the labels from the problem:

> REMEMBER THAT:
> *miles per hour*
> means the ratio
> $\frac{miles}{hour}$

$$\text{miles} \ \square \ \text{hours} = \frac{miles}{hour}$$

How would you fill in the box? Ask yourself, "What do I have to do to *miles* and *hours* in order to get $\frac{miles}{hour}$?" You need to divide:

$$385 \text{ miles} \ \boxed{\div} \ 7 \text{ hours} = \frac{\textbf{55 miles}}{\textbf{hour}}$$

OR

$$385 \text{ miles} \div 7 \text{ hours} = \textbf{55 miles per hour}$$

Now look at the next example:

Example 4:   Ken took a 7-hour trip. He averaged 55 miles per hour on the trip. How many miles in all did he drive?

The label of one piece of the necessary information is *hours*; the label of the other piece is *miles per hour*. The label of the answer will be *miles*. Ask yourself, "What would I do to *hours* and *miles per hour* to get *miles*?"

$$\text{hours} \ \square \ \frac{miles}{hour} = \text{miles}$$

Try multiplying. Just as with numerical multiplication, you can cancel out common factors (in this case, the label *hour*):

canceling
using words

canceling
using numbers

$$\cancel{\text{hours}} \ \boxed{\times} \ \frac{miles}{\cancel{hour}} = \text{miles} \qquad \qquad \cancel{5} \times \frac{3}{\cancel{5}} = 3$$

Because canceling labels leaves you the label to your answer, you know that you should multiply to get the correct answer:

$$\text{\sout{hours}} \ \square \ \frac{\text{miles}}{\text{\sout{hour}}} = \text{miles}$$

$$7 \ \text{\sout{hours}} \ \boxtimes \ \frac{55 \ \text{miles}}{1 \ \text{\sout{hour}}} = ? \ \text{miles}$$

$$7 \ \text{hours} \times 55 \ \text{mph} = \textbf{385 miles}$$

Now, look at a problem in which you can't cancel the labels.

Example 5:   Ken took a 385-mile trip and drove 55 miles per hour. How many hours did he drive?

Look at the expression: $\text{miles} \ \square \ \dfrac{\text{miles}}{\text{hour}} = \text{hours}$

Can you convert the labels to a common unit? No. Can you cancel the labels *miles* and *hours*? No. When you can't cancel the labels, try dividing.

$$385 \ \text{miles} \ \boxdot \ \frac{55 \ \text{miles}}{1 \ \text{hour}} = ? \ \text{hours}$$

$$385 \ \text{miles} \ \boxdot \ 55 \ \text{mph} = \textbf{7 hours}$$

Try the next exercise. As with any new problem-solving technique, the more you practice it, the easier it will become.

• • • • • • • •
Exercise 2

Part A

Read each of the following problems. Look at the labels and decide if they can be renamed to a broader category. Then write in the correct operation to solve the problem. Finally, solve the problem.

1.   Sam cut an 8-ounce slice from a 20-pound round of cheese. How many ounces of cheese were left?

necessary information labels: _____ _____

answer label: _____

Are the labels different? ____ Yes ____

If so, what is the new label? ouncES ____

_____ $\square$ _____ = _____
label   label   label

Answer: _____

2. Adrienne needed to cut 2 feet from a 72-inch piece of molding. After the cut, how much molding was left?

necessary information labels: _____ _____

answer label: _____

Are the labels different? _____

If so, what is the new label? _____

_____ ☐ _____ = _____
    label   label   label

Answer: _____

3. Maura's hair was $9\frac{1}{2}$ inches long. How long was her hair before she had cut it by $1\frac{3}{4}$ inches?

necessary information labels: _____ _____

answer label: _____

Are the labels different? _____

If so, what is the new label? _____

_____ ☐ _____ = _____
    label   label   label

Answer: _____

Part B

Read the following problems. First look at the labels in the problem and see if they can be canceled. Then write the correct operation in the box. Finally, solve the problem.

1. A ream of paper contains 500 sheets. A box contains 10 reams of paper. How many sheets of paper are in the box?

$\frac{\text{sheets}}{\text{ream}}$ ☐ reams = sheets   Answer: _____

2. It cost $6 to go to the movies. A movie theater collected $522 in ticket sales. How many tickets were sold?

dollars ☐ $\frac{\text{dollars}}{\text{ticket}}$ = tickets   Answer: _____

3. An average tomato plant in John's garden yields 8 pounds of tomatoes. How much of a harvest should he expect from his 14 tomato plants?

plants ☐ $\frac{\text{pounds}}{\text{plant}}$ = pounds   Answer: _____

Answers on page 176.

NOT ENOUGH INFORMATION

Now that you know how to decide whether to add, subtract, multiply, or divide to solve a word problem, you should be able to recognize a word problem that cannot be solved because not enough information is given.

Look at the following example:

Example 1: At her waitress job, Sheila earns $4.50 an hour plus tips. Last week she got $65.40 in tips. How much did she earn last week?

  Step 1: *question:* How much did she earn last week?
  Step 2: *necessary information:* $4.50/hour, $65.40
  Step 3: *decide what arithmetic to use:*

tips + (pay per hour × hours worked) = total earned

missing information: hours worked

At first glance, you might think that you have enough information since there are 2 numbers. But when the solution is set up, you can see that you need to know the number of hours Sheila worked to find out what she earned.

•••••••
Exercise 3

For each word problem, circle the letter of the correct answer.

1. A supermarket sold 350 pounds of bananas at $.59 a pound. How many pounds of bananas did it have left?

  a. *You need to know how much the supermarket paid for the bananas.*
  b. *You need to know how many pounds of bananas the supermarket started with.*
  c. *You need to know how much money the supermarket made for each pound of bananas sold.*
  d. *You have enough information to solve the problem.*

2. In one day last year, 2,417 people were born or moved into the state and 1,620 people died or left the state. What was the state's change of population for the day?

   a. *You need to know the total population of the state.*
   b. *You need to know the name of the state.*
   c. *You need to know exactly how many people were born and exactly how many died.*
   d. *You have enough information to solve the problem.*

3. Roast beef that normally costs $2.59 a pound was marked down $.60. If Gina paid for a roast with a $10.00 bill, how much change did she receive?

   a. *You need to know the weight of Gina's roast beef.*
   b. *You need to know the total amount of money Gina had.*
   c. *You need to know how much the supermarket paid for the roast beef.*
   d. *You have enough information to solve the problem.*

4. A loaded truck carrying boxes of books weighed 7,105 pounds at the weigh station. If each box of books weighed 42 pounds, how much did the unloaded truck weigh?

   a. *You need to know how many books were in the truck.*
   b. *You need to know the weight of a single book.*
   c. *You need to know how many boxes were in the truck.*
   d. *You have enough information to solve the problem.*

5. A bag of 40 snack bars weighs 12 ounces. How much does each snack bar weigh?

   a. *You need to know the price of 1 snack bar.*
   b. *You need to know how many ounces are in a pound.*
   c. *You need to know the total price of the entire bag.*
   d. *You have enough information to solve the problem.*

Answers on page 177.

Exercise 4

In the following problems, decide whether to add, subtract, multiply, or divide. Then solve the problem. Circle the letter of the correct answer.

1. Mr. Gomez's obituary appeared in a 1983 newspaper. It said that he was 86 years old when he died and had been married for 51 years. In what year was he born?

    a. *1903*
    b. *1932*
    c. *1869*
    d. *1887*
    e. *1897*

2. An electrician has a piece of cable the length shown at right. How long a cable would he have if he laid 7 of these pieces end to end?

    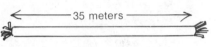

    a. *5 meters*
    b. *28 meters*
    c. *42 meters*
    d. *245 meters*
    e. *490 meters*

3. The population of San Jose rose by 37,290 people. The population had been 596,640. What was the new population?

    a. *559,350 people*
    b. *633,930 people*
    c. *160,000 people*
    d. *180,500 people*
    e. *not enough information is given*

4. A Christmas light uses 2 watts of electricity. How many lights can be strung on a circuit that can handle a load of 300 watts?

    a. *150 lights*
    b. *600 lights*
    c. *298 lights*
    d. *302 lights*
    e. *none of the above*

5. A telephone cable can handle 12,500 calls at any one time.
    How many cables are needed to handle a peak load of 87,500
    calls?

    a. *100,000 cables*
    b. *75,000 cables*
    c. *7 cables*
    d. *70 cables*
    e. *none of the above*

6. Gene bought $360 worth of sports equipment and $18 worth
    of office supplies for the boys' club. Since the boys' club is
    tax-exempt, he didn't have to pay the sales tax. If he had
    paid tax, how much would he have spent?

    a. *$20*
    b. *$378*
    c. *$342*
    d. *$360*
    e. *not enough information is given*

7. A clothing factory produced 8,760 yards of cloth. What was
    the average production from each of the 60 looms in the
    factory?

    a. *146 yards*
    b. *1,460 yards*
    c. *8,700 yards*
    d. *8,820 yards*
    e. *525,600 yards*

8. Len's goal was to sell 20 encyclopedias a month. Part of
    Len's sales log is shown at right. By how much did he
    exceed his goal in September?

    a. *57 encyclopedias*
    b. *17 encyclopedias*
    c. *13 encyclopedias*
    d. *2 encyclopedias*
    e. *740 encyclopedias*

Encyclopedia Sales	
August	19
September	37
October	30
November	21

Answers on page 177.

MIXED WORD PROBLEMS—WHOLE NUMBERS, DECIMALS, AND FRACTIONS

Exercise 5

For all problems, circle the letter of the correct answer. Round off decimals to the nearest penny or the nearest hundredth.

1. Sandy bought a roast beef sandwich for $1.89, which included $.09 tax. What was the cost of the sandwich alone?

    a. $1.89
    b. $1.80
    c. $1.98
    d. $2.10
    e. $1.70

2. The population of the United States was 253,478,921. The population of the Soviet Union was 281,300,845. How much greater was the population of the Soviet Union than the population of the United States?

    a. 27,821,924 people
    b. 534,779,766 people
    c. 32,178,124 people
    d. 534,778,766 people
    e. none of the above

3. To tie her tomato plants, Emmy cut the string shown at right into $\frac{3}{4}$-foot-long pieces. How many pieces of string did she have to tie her tomatoes?

    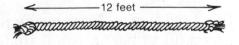

    a. $12\frac{3}{4}$ feet
    b. $11\frac{1}{4}$ feet
    c. 9 pieces
    d. 16 pieces
    e. none of the above

4. Chicken costs $.65 a pound. Cali paid $2.90 for a chicken. How much did the chicken weigh? (Round to nearest hundredth.)

    a. 2.25 pounds
    b. 2.35 pounds
    c. 1.89 pounds
    d. 4.46 pounds
    e. 18.9 pounds

5. A strobe light flashes every $\frac{1}{250}$ of a second. How many times does it flash in 5 seconds?

    a. *50 times*

    b. *1,250 times*

    c. $4\frac{249}{250}$ *times*

    d. $5\frac{1}{250}$ *times*

    e. *not enough information is given*

6. Debbie spent $\frac{1}{3}$ of her paycheck on food and $\frac{1}{4}$ for clothes. Her paycheck was for $138. How much did she spend for food?

    a. *$46.00*

    b. *$51.40*

    c. *$80.50*

    d. *$5.14*

    e. *$34.50*

7. The city school system planned to lay off 216 teachers and 85 aides. How many people was the school system planning to lay off?

    a. *131 people*

    b. *171 people*

    c. *301 people*

    d. *271 people*

    e. *3 people*

8. Lori won a Megabucks jackpot of $2,478,000 that will be paid to her in equal installments each year for 30 years. How much will she receive each year?

    a. *$82,600*

    b. *$74,340,000*

    c. *$678,000*

    d. *$2,478,030*

    e. *$2,478,970*

9. To fit into a groove, a board must be $\frac{13}{16}$ inch thick. How much of the board shown at right must be sanded off for it to fit in the groove?

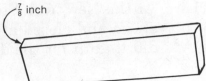

$\frac{7}{8}$ inch

   a. $\frac{3}{4}$ inch

   b. $\frac{5}{6}$ inch

   c. $1\frac{1}{13}$ inches

   d. $1\frac{11}{16}$ inches

   e. $\frac{1}{16}$ inch

10. Rene had to ship a 3.6-pound package. Overnight Delivery Service charged $1.16 per pound for delivery. How much did Rene pay to get her package delivered? (Round off to the nearest penny.)

   a. $4.76

   b. $2.44

   c. $2.56

   d. $4.18

   e. $3.10

11. A factory produces 4-ton steel girders. How much steel does the factory need to produce 1,200 of these girders?

   a. 300 tons

   b. 4,800 tons

   c. 1,204 tons

   d. 1,196 tons

   e. not enough information is given

12. Yesterday, after buying 9 gallons of gasoline, Mimi drove 108 miles. How many miles per gallon does her car get?

   a. 972 miles

   b. 12 miles per gallon

   c. 99 miles per gallon

   d. 117 miles

   e. not enough information is given

13. Harry sanded $\frac{1}{6}$ of a floor. Fran sanded $\frac{1}{4}$ of the floor. How much of the floor got sanded?

   a. $\frac{1}{5}$ of the floor

   b. $\frac{2}{3}$ of the floor

   c. $\frac{5}{12}$ of the floor

   d. $\frac{1}{12}$ of the floor

   e. $\frac{1}{24}$ of the floor

14. At the New York Stock Market, a stock opened at $20\frac{3}{8}$ a
    share and closed at the end of the day at $22\frac{1}{2}$. How much
    did it gain for the day?

    a. $42\frac{7}{8}$
    b. $2\frac{1}{8}$
    c. $2\frac{1}{3}$
    d. $2\frac{2}{5}$
    e. *none of the above*

15. What is the total weight of the two packages of fruit shown
    at right?

    a. *1.81 pounds*
    b. *1.63 pounds*
    c. *2.62 pounds*
    d. *1.55 pounds*
    e. *.82 pound*

PEACHES   1.72 lb.   PLUMS   .9 lb.

16. A serving of Kellogg's Raisin Bran contains .26 grams of
    potassium. How many grams of potassium are in an 11-
    serving package of Raisin Bran?

    a. *11.26 grams*
    b. *10.74 grams*
    c. *42.31 grams*
    d. *2.86 grams*
    e. *.02 gram*

Answers on page 177.

• • • • • • • •
Exercise 6

For all problems, circle the letter of the correct answer. Round
off decimals to the nearest penny or the nearest hundredth.

1. The auto repair shop charged Muriel $1,125 to repair her
   car. She had a $250-deductible insurance policy. How much
   did the insurance company pay for the repair of her car?

   a. *$1,375.00*
   b. *$875.00*
   c. *$4.50*
   d. *$281.25*
   e. *none of the above*

2. Amanda packed 16 ounces of dried chives into bottles the size shown at right. How many bottles did she use?

$3\frac{1}{2}$ inches

  a. *10 bottles*
  b. *25 bottles*
  c. *$16\frac{5}{8}$ bottles*
  d. *56 bottles*
  e. *none of the above*

3. State Airlines does a complete maintenance check of its airplanes every 12,000 miles flown. Airplane #200 was flown 96,000 miles last year. How many complete maintenance checks did it have last year?

  a. *480 maintenance checks*
  b. *84,000 miles*
  c. *108,000 miles*
  d. *8 maintenance checks*
  e. *1,152,000,000 miles*

4. After getting a tune-up, Ernie was able to drive 283.1 miles on 14.9 gallons of gas. How many miles did he get per gallon?

  a. *19 miles*
  b. *42.18 miles*
  c. *134 miles*
  d. *298 miles*
  e. *268.2 miles*

5. The Platte River is normally 7 feet deep. During a recent flood, it crested at 14 feet above normal. What was the depth of the river at the crest of the flood?

  a. *7 feet*
  b. *21 feet*
  c. *98 feet*
  d. *2 feet*
  e. *none of the above*

6. The *Concorde* flew 3,855 miles across the Atlantic in $3\frac{3}{4}$ hours. What was its average speed?

  a. *$3,858\frac{3}{4}$ miles per hour*
  b. *$3,851\frac{1}{4}$ miles per hour*
  c. *1,028 miles per hour*
  d. *$14,456\frac{1}{3}$ miles per hour*
  e. *$467\frac{9}{33}$ miles per hour*

7. After paying an average of $980 a year for taxes over the past 5 years, Francine's taxes jumped to $2,420 this year. How much more did she pay this year than she had on the average for the past 5 years?

    a. *$1,440*
    b. *$4,900*
    c. *$3,400*
    d. *$484*
    e. *$975*

8. Maura bought 6 compact discs for $83.88. Then she bought a carrying case. How much did she spend?

    a. *$13.98*
    b. *$89.99*
    c. *$503.28*
    d. *$76.88*
    e. *not enough information is given*

9. A stick of butter weighs $\frac{1}{4}$ pound. A recipe calls for $\frac{1}{2}$ stick of butter. How many pounds of butter are needed?

    a. *2 pounds*
    b. *$\frac{3}{4}$ pound*
    c. *$\frac{1}{4}$ pound*
    d. *$\frac{1}{8}$ pound*
    e. *$\frac{1}{2}$ pound*

10. Kendra deposited $28 in her account every week for a year. How much money did she deposit in the account?

    a. *$24*
    b. *$80*
    c. *$336*
    d. *$1,456*
    e. *not enough information is given*

11. A public television station expected private contributions to pay for $\frac{2}{3}$ of its expenses. Before the end-of-year appeal, these contributions totaled only enough to pay for $\frac{4}{9}$ of expenses. How much more must be raised?

    a. *$\frac{2}{9}$ of expenses*
    b. *$\frac{1}{2}$ of expenses*
    c. *$\frac{1}{3}$ of expenses*
    d. *$\frac{6}{27}$ of expenses*
    e. *$\frac{2}{3}$ of expenses*

12. Ronica, a buyer for a major supermarket, paid $.38 a pound for the shipment of grapefruits shown at right. How much did she pay for the shipment?

   a. *$760.38*
   b. *$798*
   c. *$2,000*
   d. *$288.80*
   e. *not enough information is given*

13. Josie spent $25 for the book *Great American Music* and then spent $2.75 for sheet music. How much did she spend?

   a. *$9.90*
   b. *$3.00*
   c. *$27.75*
   d. *$68.75*
   e. *$22.25*

14. A newsboy sold 304 newspapers. If each newspaper costs $.35, how much money did he collect?

   a. *$106.40*
   b. *$86.86*
   c. *$304.35*
   d. *$303.65*
   e. *none of the above*

15. A bunch of grapes weighed 1.84 pounds. Another bunch of grapes weighed 2.2 pounds. How much heavier was the second bunch of grapes?

   a. *1.62 pounds*
   b. *2.06 pounds*
   c. *4.05 pounds*
   d. *4.04 pounds*
   e. *.36 pound*

16. A 28-gram serving of Quaker Chewy Granola Bars has 2 grams of protein. How much protein is there in a single gram of the granola bar?

   a. *14 grams*
   b. *30 grams*
   c. *26 grams*
   d. *56 grams*
   e. *.07 gram*

Answers on page 178.

Chapter 9

Percent Word Problems

IDENTIFYING THE PARTS OF A PERCENT WORD PROBLEM

Read the statement below:

The 8-ounce glass is 50% full. It contains 4 ounces.

This statement contains 3 facts:

the whole: the 8-ounce glass
the part: 4 ounces
the percent: 50%

A percent word problem would be missing one of these facts. When you are solving a percent word problem, the first step is to identify what you are looking for. As shown above, you have 3 possible choices: *the part*, *the whole*, or *the percent*.

It is usually easiest to figure out that you are being asked to find the percent. Word problems asking for the percent usually ask for it directly, with a question such as "What is the percent?" or "Find the percent" or "3 is what percent?" Occasionally, other percent-type words are used, such as "What is the *interest rate*?"

Example 1: 6 is what percent of 30?

The question asks, "is what percent?" Therefore, you are looking for the percent.

Sometimes you are given the percent and 1 other number. You must decide whether you are looking for the part or the whole.

Example 2: 81% of what number is 162?

The phrase "of what number" means you are looking for the whole.

Example 3:   114 city employees were absent yesterday. This was 4% of the city work force. How many people work for the city?

Step 1:   *question:* How many people work for the city?

Step 2:   *necessary information:* 114 city employees, 4%

Step 3:   You are given the number of city employees who were absent (114) and the percent of the work force that this represents (4%). You are looking for the total number of people who work for the city, the whole.

Example 4:   What number is 75% of 40?

You are looking for a number that is a percent of another number. You are looking for the part.

Example 5:   Operating at full capacity, the automobile plant produced 25 cars an hour. How many cars did the plant produce when operating at 40% capacity?

Step 1:   *question:* How many cars did the plant produce?

Step 2:   *necessary information:* 25 cars, 40%

Step 3:   You are given the production at full capacity (25 cars an hour). To find the production at 40% capacity, you must solve for the part.

• • • • • • • •
Exercise 1

For each problem, write down whether you are looking for the part, the whole, or the percent. DO NOT SOLVE!

1.   The city reported that 14,078 out of 35,817 registered voters voted in the election. What percent of the registered voters voted in the election?

   _____

2.   A total of 14,615 people voted in the election. The election results are shown at right. How many votes did the winning candidate get?

   _____

Vote Percentages	
Candidate A	54%
Candidate B	39%
Candidate C	7%

3. 36% of the plumbers polled recommended Drāno. 72 plumbers recommended Drāno. How many plumbers were polled?

    _____

4. 85% of Eric's roll of 36 pictures were perfect prints. How many perfect prints did he get from the roll?

    _____

5. A seed company guaranteed 87% germination of its spinach seed. If Jed had 450 spinach seeds germinate, how many seeds did he plant?

    _____

6. The state had a work force of 1,622,145. 132,998 of those people were unemployed. What was the unemployment rate for the state?

    _____

7. A bedroom set normally priced at $1,400 is on sale. How much would Rochelle save if she bought the set at the advertised sale, shown at right, instead of at the regular price?

    _____

    FURNITURE SALE
    ALL BEDROOM SETS
    40% OFF

8. Last year, 980 people took the high school equivalency exam at the local official test center. 637 people passed the exam. What percent of the people taking the exam passed?

    _____

9. If 8% of the registered voters sign the initiative petition, it will be placed on the November ballot. There are 193,825 registered voters in the county. How many of them must sign the petition for it to go on the ballot?

    _____

10. An independent study group estimated that only 35% of all crimes in the city were reported. 2,800 crimes were reported last year. According to the study, how many crimes were actually committed?

    _____

Answers on page 178.

SOLVING PERCENT WORD PROBLEMS

Once you identify what you are looking for in a percent word problem, set up the problem and solve it.

Percent word problems can be solved using proportions. These problems can be set up in the following form:

$$\frac{\text{part}}{\text{whole}} = \frac{\%}{100\%}$$

Using the proportion method, you can solve for 1 of 3 numbers: the part, the whole, or the percent. The percent is always written over 100 because the percent represents a fraction with 100 in the denominator.

As you saw in your earlier work with proportions, a proportion is the same as 2 equivalent fractions. For example,

2 is 50% of 4 and can be written as

$$\frac{2}{4} = \frac{50\%}{100\%}$$

2 is the *part*, 4 is the *whole*, and 50 is the *percent*.

Example 1: 4 is what percent of 16?

Step 1: *question:* is what percent?

You are looking for the percent.

Step 2: *necessary information:* 4 is, of 16

For this type of percent exercise, the word *is* follows the part, and the number after *of* is the whole.

Step 3: Set up a proportion in this form:

$$\underset{\text{numbers}}{\underbrace{\frac{\text{part}}{\text{whole}}}} = \underset{\text{percents}}{\underbrace{\frac{\text{percent}}{100}}}$$

Fill in the proportion with the given information from the problem. Call the number you are looking for *n*.

$$\underset{\text{numbers}}{\frac{4}{16}} = \underset{\text{percents}}{\frac{n}{100}}$$

Step 4: Cross multiply: $16 \times n = 4 \times 100$

$$16n = 400$$

Divide: $n = \dfrac{400}{16} = \mathbf{25\%}$

Example 2: 24 out of 96 city playgrounds needed major repairs. What percent of the city playgrounds needed major repairs?

Step 1: *question:* What percent of the city playgrounds needed major repairs?

You are looking for the percent.

Step 2: *necessary information:* 24 out of 96

96 is the whole (all the playgrounds).
24 is the part (playgrounds needing repairs).

Step 3:
$$\underline{\quad numbers \quad} \qquad \underline{\quad percents \quad}$$

$$\frac{24 \text{ playgrounds}}{96 \text{ playgrounds}} = \frac{n}{100}$$

Step 4: Cross multiply: $96 \times n = 24 \times 100$

$$96n = 2{,}400$$

Divide: $n = \dfrac{2{,}400}{96} = \mathbf{25\%}$

Example 3: 30% of what number is 78?

Step 1: *question:* of what number?

You are looking for the whole.

Step 2: *necessary information:* 30%, is 78

30% is the percent.
78 is the part.

Step 3: Set up a proportion in this form:

$$\frac{78}{n} = \frac{30}{100}$$

Step 4: Cross multiply: $30 \times n = 78 \times 100$

$$30n = 7{,}800$$

Divide: $n = \dfrac{7{,}800}{30} = \mathbf{260}$

Example 4:   The finance company required that Lynn make a down payment of 15% on a used car. She can afford a down payment of $600. What is the most expensive car that she could buy?

Step 1:   *question:* What is the most expensive car that she could buy?

You are looking for the whole (the price of the car).

Step 2:   *necessary information:* 15%, $600

15% is the percent.
$600 is the down payment, which is a part of the total price of the car.

Step 3: $\dfrac{\$600}{\$n} = \dfrac{15}{100}$

Step 4:   Cross multiply: $15 \times n = 600 \times 100$

$$15n = 60{,}000$$

Divide: $n = \dfrac{60{,}000}{15} = \mathbf{\$4{,}000}$

Example 5:   What is 40% of 65?

Step 1:   *question:* What is?

You are looking for the part.

Step 2:   *necessary information:* 40%, of 65

40% is the percent.
65 is the whole.

Step 3:   Set up a proportion in this form:

$$\dfrac{n}{65} = \dfrac{40}{100}$$

Step 4:   Cross multiply: $100 \times n = 65 \times 40$

$$100n = 2{,}600$$

Divide: $n = \dfrac{2{,}600}{100} = \mathbf{26}$

Example 6:   June decided that she could spend 25% of her income for rent. She makes $580 a month. How much can she spend for rent?

Step 1:   *question:* How much can she spend for rent?

You are looking for the part of her income that she will spend on rent.

Step 2:   *necessary information:* 25%, $580

25% is the percent.
$580 is her whole income.

Step 3:   *proportion:*

$$\frac{\$n}{\$580} = \frac{25}{100}$$

Step 4:   Cross multiply: $100 \times n = 580 \times 25$

$$100n = 14{,}500$$

Divide: $n = \dfrac{14{,}500}{100} = \textbf{\$145}$

Exercise 2

Solve the following problems by using proportions.

1. 36 is what percent of 144?

2. 288 is 72% of what number?

3. What is 68% of 75?

4. A $160 suit was reduced by $40. What was the percent of the reduction?

5. The election results are shown at right. 28,450 votes were cast in the school board election. How many votes did Marsha receive?

6. The state government cut aid for adult education by 25%. Metropolis expects to lose $96,000. How much aid for adult education had Metropolis been receiving?

7. Last year Jeffrey paid 7% of his income in taxes. He paid $553. What was his income?

School Board Elections	
Clayton	19%
Andrea	21%
Marcus	2%
Marsha	58%

8. 60% of the residents of the city are African-American. The population of the city is 345,780. How many African-American people live in the city?

9. In 1982, Robyn paid $340 interest on $2,000 that she had borrowed. What was the interest rate on the borrowed money?

Answers on page 178.

SOLVING PERCENT WORD PROBLEMS INVOLVING DECIMALS AND FRACTIONS

Many percent word problems also contain decimals or fractions. These problems are also solved using the proportion method.

Example 1: What is $33\frac{1}{3}\%$ of 54?

Step 1: *question:* What is?

You are looking for the part.

Step 2: *necessary information:* $33\frac{1}{3}\%$, of 54

$33\frac{1}{3}$ is the percent.
54 is the whole.

Step 3: *proportion:*

$$\frac{n}{54} = \frac{33\frac{1}{3}}{100}$$

Step 4: Cross multiply and divide: $100 \times n = 33\frac{1}{3} \times 54$

$$100n = 1,800$$

$$n = \frac{1,800}{100} = \mathbf{18}$$

Example 2: Bob takes home $156.40 out of his weekly pay of $184. What percent of his pay does he take home?

Step 1: *question:* What percent of his pay does he take home?

You are looking for the percent.

Step 2: *necessary information:* $156.40, $184

$156.40 is the part.
$184 is the whole.

Step 3: *proportion*:

$$\frac{\$156.40}{\$184} = \frac{n}{100}$$

Step 4: Cross multiply and divide: $184 \times n = 156.40 \times 100$

$$184n = 15,640$$

$$n = \frac{15,640}{184} = \mathbf{85\%}$$

• • • • • • • •

Exercise 3

Solve the following percent problems using proportions.

1. 4.5% of what number is 90? _____

2. $\frac{1}{10}$ is what percent of $\frac{3}{4}$? _____

3. $66\frac{2}{3}\%$ of what number is 42? _____

4. What is 6.4% of 800?   _____

5. Russo's Restaurant collected $49.76 in taxes Friday night. The food tax is 8%. How much money did the restaurant receive for meals on Friday night?

    _____

6. Jed bought a steak dinner for $8.60. Using the tax chart at right, find the amount of tax he paid.

    _____

State Tax Guidelines
Clothing—6%
Food—5%
Alcohol—7%
Cigarettes—8%

7. Glenda bought maple syrup for $1.92 a pint and sold the syrup for $.96 a pint more. By what percent did she mark up the price of the maple syrup?

    _____

8. Barnes and Noble was having a storewide book sale in which all prices were cut $12\frac{1}{2}\%$. How much did Juan save on a book that normally costs $12.80?

    _____

Answers on page 179.

PERCENT WORD PROBLEM REVIEW

The following problems give you a chance to review percent word problems containing whole numbers, decimals, and fractions.

• • • • • • • •
Exercise 4

Solve the problems by using proportions.

1. 3 out of 4 dentists recommend a fluoride toothpaste. What percent of all dentists recommend a fluoride toothpaste?

    _____

2. 112,492 people voted for mayor in the city. This was 40% of the registered voters. How many registered voters are there in the city?

    _____

3. In a normal season, the Seaside Resort has 34,500 visitors. This year, due to bad weather, 11,500 fewer visitors came to the resort. What was the percent drop in business for the resort?

    _____

4. The High Tech Electronics Company announced an 8.6% profit on sales of $49,600,000. How much profit did the company make?

    _____

5. The Quality Chocolate Company decided to increase the size of its chocolate bar .4 ounce. This was an increase in size of $16\frac{2}{3}$%. What was the weight of its chocolate bar before the change?

    _____

6. In a recent flu epidemic, .8% of people over age 65 who caught the disease died. The death toll in this group was 40. How many people over age 65 caught the flu?

    _____

7. In 1990, Dennis paid 13% of his income in taxes. How much did he pay in income taxes that year according to the chart at right?

_____

Yearly Earnings Dennis Ferguson
1989—$10,048
1990—$11,694
1991—$12,509

8. The Machinist's Union has just won a 7% raise for its members. Dan is a union member who was making $17,548. How much of a raise will he get?

_____

9. Nayana received a 9% raise worth $18 a week. What had her week's salary been?

_____

10. Basketball star Kareem scored on 506 out of 1,012 attempts. What was his scoring percentage?

_____

11. A $\frac{3}{4}$-cup serving of Honey Nut Cheerios served with skim milk provides 30% of the U.S. recommended daily allowance of vitamin A. How many cups of Honey Nut Cheerios must you eat in order to receive the full U.S. recommended daily allowance of vitamin A when you have skim milk with each serving?

_____

12. A $3\frac{3}{4}$-ounce serving of Norway Sardines in Chili Sauce provides 100% of the U.S. recommended daily allowance for vitamin D. What percent of the U.S. daily allowance is provided per ounce of the Norway Sardines in Chili Sauce?

_____

Answers on page 180.

Chapter 10

Combination Word Problems

SOLVING COMBINATION WORD PROBLEMS

Until now, this book has shown you 1-step word problems. However, many situations require you to use a combination of math operations to solve word problems.

Generally, you can solve these combination problems by breaking them into 2 or more 1-step problems. As you read a word problem, you may see that it will take more than 1 math operation to solve. The difficulty lies in deciding how many steps to take and in what order to work them out.

The key to solving combination problems is:

Start with the question and work backward.

This shouldn't be difficult. Throughout this book, you have started your work with finding the question.

These are the steps in solving combination word problems:

Step 1: Find the question.
Step 2: Select the necessary information.
Step 3: Write a solution sentence for the problem. Fill in only the necessary information that belongs in the solution sentence.
Write another sentence, this time to find the information that is missing in the solution sentence. Solve the sentence that gives you the missing information.
Step 4: Fill in the missing information (the answer from Step 3) in the solution sentence and solve.
Step 5: Make sure that the answer is sensible.

No matter how many short problems a combination problem consists of, you can always work backward from the solution sentence. Examples 1 and 2 illustrate this.

Example 1: Sengchen had $38 in her checking account. She wrote checks for $14 and $9. How much money was left in her checking account?

Step 1: *question:* How much money was left in her checking account?

Step 2: *necessary information:* $38, $14, $9

Step 3: Write a solution sentence.

money − checks = money left

Fill in the sentence with information that can be used to solve the problem.

$38 −checks=money left

Decide what *missing information* is needed to solve the problem. Write a number sentence and solve.

check + check = checks

$14 + $9 = $\boxed{$23}$

$38 − $\boxed{$23}$ =money left

Now you have the complete information needed to solve the problem.

Step 4: Solve.

$38 −$23 =$15 left

Example 2: Lillie worked as a travel agent. She arranged a trip for 56 people at a cost of $165 for airfare plus $230 for hotel per person. How much money did she collect from the group?

Step 1: *question:* How much money did she collect?

Step 2: *necessary information:* 56 people, $165 airfare, $230 hotel accommodations

Step 3: Write a solution sentence:

cost × number of people = total

cost x 56= total

solve for *missing information:*

airfare + hotel = cost

$165 + $230 = $\boxed{$395}$

$\boxed{$395}$ x 56 =total cost
$395 x 56 =$22,120 total

Step 4: Solve.

The words that you use in the solution and missing information sentences may differ from what we have here. What is important is that you break down the problem into smaller steps.

A combination word problem that needs both multiplication and division to be solved can often be written as 1 proportion instead of 2 separate word sentences. If you need to review writing and solving proportions, see Chapter 7: Using Proportions.

Example 3: Apples were sold at a cost of 58 cents for 2 pounds. How much did Michelle pay for 3 pounds of apples?

Step 1: *question:* How much did Michelle pay for 3 pounds of apples?

Step 2: *necessary information:* 2 pounds, 58 cents, 3 pounds

Step 3: Write a proportion to show the relationship between weight and cost.

Step 4: Fill in the appropriate numbers and solve.

$$\frac{pounds}{cents} = \frac{pounds}{cents}$$

$$\frac{2\ pounds}{58\ cents} = \frac{3\ pounds}{n}$$

$$2 \times n = 3 \times 58$$

$$n = \frac{174}{2} = 87\ cents$$

After some practice, you will be able to tell which problems can be solved with a proportion. In most cases, breaking down a problem into smaller problems with word sentences will be the best method for solution.

• • • • • • • •
Exercise 1

For each word problem, write 2 word sentences (a solution sentence and a missing information sentence) or a proportion. DO NOT SOLVE!

1. Tim earns $230 a week. Every week, $49 in taxes and $6 in union dues are taken out of his paycheck. What is his take-home pay?

    _____

    _____

2. After starting the day with $41, Miguel spent $3 for lunch and $22 for gas. How much money did he have left by the end of the day?

    _____

    _____

3. Samuel had $394 in his checking account. After he wrote a check for $187 and deposited $201, how much money was in his checking account?

_____

_____

4. Kelly bought 5 of the blouses shown at right and 1 of the skirts. How much money did she spend on these clothes?

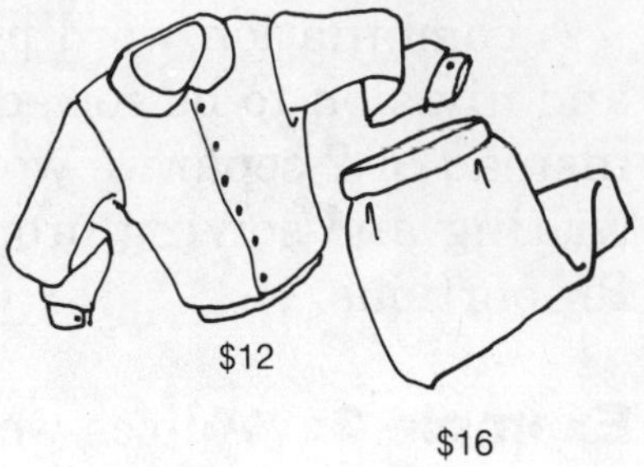

_____

_____

$12

$16

5. Martha borrowed $4,600 to buy a new car. She will have to pay $728 interest. She plans to pay back the loan plus the interest in 24 equal monthly payments. How much will her monthly payments be?

_____

_____

6. A store bought 30 boxes of dolls for $720. If there were 8 dolls in a box, how much did each doll cost?

_____

_____

7. At the candy counter, licorice cost 5 cents for 3 pieces. Cindy gave her daughter Emily 30 cents to spend on licorice. How many pieces of licorice was Emily able to buy?

_____

_____

8. Jocelyn bought a skirt for $14 and a blouse for $9. She paid for the clothes with a $100 bill. What was her change?

_____

_____

9. To be hired, a data entry operator must be able to enter numbers into a computer at the rate of 10,000 numbers every 60 minutes. Yvana took a 15-minute data entry test. How many numbers did she have to enter to be hired?

_____

_____

10. A school needs to determine how many square feet of carpet to order for three rooms. How many square feet of carpeting must be ordered if each room is the size shown at right?

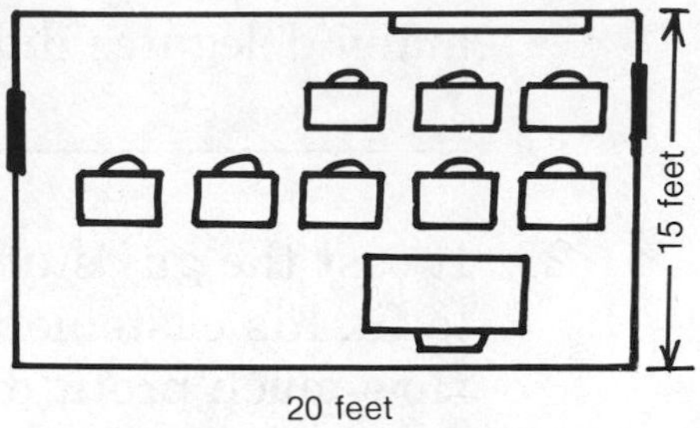

_____

_____

11. Dara had 2 quarters, 1 dime, 4 nickels, and 7 pennies in her change purse. After putting 65 cents in a vending machine, how much change did she have left?

_____

_____

12. A 14-gram serving of Cain's Mayonnaise contains 5 grams of polyunsaturated fat and 2 grams of saturated fat. How many grams of saturated fat are there in a 224-gram jar of Cain's Mayonnaise?

_____

_____

Answers on page 181.

• • • • • • •
Exercise 2

Write the two 1-step word sentences or the proportion needed to solve the following combination word problems. Then solve the problems.

1. For the convention, each of the 8 wards of the city elected 4 delegates, while 5 delegates were elected at large. How many delegates did the city send to the convention?

    _____

2. It cost the gas station owner $81 in parts and $45 in labor to fix his customer's car. He charged his customer $163. How much profit did the owner make on the job?

    _____

3. After working at the copying machine for 5 minutes, Angie had made 30 copies. If she continued working at the same rate, how many copies would she make in an hour (60 minutes)?

    _____

4. 4 friends evenly split the $216 it cost to drive a car to Florida. Jennifer then spent $114 on her own for the rest of her vacation. How much did Jennifer spend on her vacation?

    _____

5. The AFL-CIO chartered buses to go to a demonstration in Washington. 4,168 union members and 1,272 other people signed up for the buses. How many buses did they have to charter if they could fit 40 people on a bus?

    _____

6. Mark was offered a job downtown that would give him a raise of $78 a month over his current salary, but his commuting costs would be $2 a day higher. If he works 22 days a month, what would be his net monthly increase in pay?

    _____

7. The recipe at right serves 6 people. Ginny is planning to make the recipe for 8 people. How much stew beef does she need?

Kay's Hearty Stew
3 cups beef stock
1 cup red wine
$\frac{1}{4}$ cup oil
2 pounds potatoes
3 pounds stew beef
1 pound carrots

_____

8. On election day, 7,481 ballots were cast at town hall. The election officials counted 4,201 votes for Chris Prelack and 2,896 for Brendan LaCerda. How many ballots were cast for a candidate other than Prelack or LaCerda?

_____

9. A 1,296-gram container of Hood Frozen Yogurt contains 2,080 calories. How many calories are in an 81-gram serving of Hood Frozen Yogurt?

_____

10. At the sale, Darlene bought 3 blouses, originally $21 each, but marked down $5 each. She also bought a pair of jeans for $23, marked down from $31. How much did she spend?

_____

Answers on page 182.

SOLVING COMBINATION WORD PROBLEMS: DECIMALS, FRACTIONS, PERCENTS

Decimal, fraction, and percent combination word problems are set up and solved in the same way as whole-number combination word problems:

Example 1: For each child at her daughter's birthday party, Shelly spent $.35 for a party favor and $.16 for a balloon. She had 13 children at the party. How much did she spend for gifts for the children?

Step 1: *question:* How much did she spend for gifts for the children?

Step 2: *necessary information:* $.35, $.16, 13 children

Step 3: *solution sentence:*

gifts × children = total cost

missing information sentence:

favor + balloon = gifts
$.35 + $.16 = $.51

gifts x 13 = total cost

$.51 x 13 = total cost
$.51 x 13 = $6.63

Step 4: Solve.

Example 2: Bright's department store advertised that everything in the store was $\frac{1}{5}$ off. Debbie bought a pair of pants labeled $20. How much did the pants cost her?

Step 1: *question:* How much did the pants cost her?

Step 2: *necessary information:* $\frac{1}{5}$, $20

Step 3: *solution sentence:*

original price − discount = sale price

missing information sentence:

price × fraction = discount
$20 × $\frac{1}{5}$ = $4 discount

$20 - discount = sale price

$20 - $4 = sale price
$20 - $4 = $16

Step 4: Solve.

Both of these examples illustrate 2-step word problems. Later in this chapter you will work with problems that need more than 2 steps for solution.

Example 3:   Real Value Hardware advertised that all prices
had been reduced 15%. A socket set is on sale for
$13.60. What was its original price?

Step 1:   *question:* What was its original price?

Step 2:   *necessary information:* 15%, $13.60

Step 3:   *solution statement:* Since this is a percent
problem, you can write a proportion.

$$\frac{\text{part}}{\text{whole}} = \frac{\text{percent}}{100}$$

missing information:

100% − *percent reduced = percent sale*
100% − 15% = 85%

Step 4:   Solve.

$$\frac{13.60}{n} = \frac{percent}{100}$$

$$\frac{13.60}{n} = \frac{85}{100}$$

$$85 \times n = 13.60 \times 100$$
$$85n = 1,360$$
$$n = \$16$$

• • • • • • • •
Exercise 3

Write the two 1-step word sentences or the proportion needed
to solve the combination word problem. Then solve the problem.

1. Chris bought 6 boxes of cookies for $14.40. If there were 20
    cookies in a box, how much did each cookie cost?

    _____

2. The $400 washing machine at right was reduced for
    clearance. What was its sale price?

    _____

3. Beverly bought 5 cans of pears, each containing $9\frac{3}{4}$ ounces
    of pears, and 1 can of fruit cocktail containing $17\frac{1}{2}$ ounces
    of fruit. What was the total weight of the fruit she bought?

    _____

4. A water widget cost Phil $2.49. Because it reduced his use
    of hot water, it saved him $3.40 a month in costs for hot
    water. What were his net savings for 12 months?

    _____

5. When cooked, a hamburger loses $\frac{1}{3}$ of its original weight. How much does a $\frac{1}{4}$-pound hamburger weigh after it is cooked?

   _____

6. The tax on a meal is 6%. How much is Milton's total bill on a $24 dinner?

   _____

7. During the summer clearance sale, everything in the store was 30% off. Solaire bought the bathing suit advertised at right. How much did she pay for the suit?

   _____

   > **30% Off the Prices Below!**
   >
   > Shorts—regularly $10.50
   > Shirts—regularly $9.00
   > Socks—regularly $1.99
   > Bathing Suits—regularly $19.50

8. Marlene bought a new couch for $310.60. She paid $130 down and planned to pay the rest in 12 equal monthly payments. How much will she pay each month?

   _____

9. Walter bought a case of 30 bottles of cooking oil for $57. He then sold the oil for $2.10 per bottle. How much money did he make on each bottle?

   _____

10. Walter bought a case of 30 bottles of cooking oil for $57. He then sold the oil for a profit of $.20 per bottle. What was the percent of profit? (Round to the nearest tenth of a percent.)

    _____

Answers on page 183.

ORDER OF OPERATIONS

You've seen how to use solution sentences to solve combination word problems. If you know and use the rules for order of operations, you can write out the steps of a multi-step word problem in 1 line.

Following are the rules for order of operations in arithmetic expressions.

Rule 1: Do multiplication and division before addition and subtraction.

Example 1: $9 - 2 \times 4$

Solution: Multiply: $2 \times 4 = 8$

Subtract: $9 - 8 = \mathbf{1}$

Example 2: $24 \div 4 + 2$

Solution: Divide: $24 \div 4 = 6$

Add: $6 + 2 = \mathbf{8}$

Rule 2: Do the arithmetic inside parentheses first.

Example 3: $(21 - 6) \div 3$

Solution: Subtract: $21 - 6 = 15$

Divide: $15 \div 3 = \mathbf{5}$

Example 4: $5 \times (4 + 8)$

Solution: Add: $4 + 8 = 12$

Multiply: $5 \times 12 = \mathbf{60}$

Rule 3: Using Rules 1 and 2, start solving arithmetic expressions from the left.

Example 5: $20 - 6 + 4$

  Solution: Subtract: $20 - 6 = 14$

              Add: $14 + 4 = \mathbf{18}$

Example 6: $1 + 2 \times 9 \div 6$

  Solution: Multiply: $2 \times 9 = 18$

              Divide: $18 \div 6 = 3$

              Add: $1 + 3 = \mathbf{4}$

Exercise 4

Using the rules for order of operations, evaluate the following arithmetic expressions.

1. $(5 \times 4) - (6 + 3)$

2. $5 \times 4 - 6 + 3$

3. $145.6 + 12.2 - 5.7 - 1.1$

4. $3.2 \times 6 + 7.8$

5. $(7.8 + 2.2) \div 5$

6. $(4 \times 9) \div 3 + 6$

7. $4 \times 9 \div 3 + 6$

8. $1.8 \div .02 - 10 - 8$

9. $1.8 \div .02 - (10 - 8)$

10. $56 - 7 \times 3.5$

Answers on page 183.

USING ORDER OF OPERATIONS IN COMBINATION WORD PROBLEMS

Look at the following examples to see how to use your knowledge of order of operations to set up a multi-step word problem.

Example 1: Frank bought dinner for 2 for $22.50. His bill was for dinner plus a 5% meal tax. What was his total bill?

Step 1: *question:* What was his total bill?

Step 2: *solution sentence:*

price of dinner + (5% × price of dinner) = total bill

Step 3:   *set up:*

$22.50 + (.05 \times 22.50) = $ total bill

Step 4:   *solution:*

Multiply: $.05 \times \$22.50 = \$1.125$

$= \$1.13$ (nearest penny)

Add: $\$22.50 + \$1.13 = \mathbf{\$23.63}$

Example 2:   Eblin lives 19 miles from work. Last week she drove to work and back 5 days and on the weekend drove 170 miles to visit relatives. How many miles did she drive last week commuting and visiting relatives?

Step 1:   *question:* How many miles did she drive?

Step 2:   *solution sentence:*

commuting + visiting relatives = total miles

Step 3:   *set up:*

(19 miles $\times$ 5 days $\times$ 2 times a day) + 170 miles = total miles

Step 4:   *solution:*

Multiply: $19 \times 5 \times 2 = 190$ miles

Add: 190 miles + 170 miles = **360 miles**

• • • • • • • •
Exercise 5

For each word problem, circle the letter of the correct setup.

1. 3 friends went out to dinner. Their meal cost $26.88. If they left a tip of $4.00, how much did each person pay if they evenly split the total amount?

    a.   *(26.88 ÷ 3) + 4.00*
    b.   *26.88 + 4.00 ÷ 3*
    c.   *26.88 + (4.00 × 3)*
    d.   *(26.88 + 4.00) ÷ 3*
    e.   *(26.88 + 4.00) × 3*

2. Kathy and Peter went clothes shopping for their baby
    daughter, Gina. They bought 5 sleepers for $8.95 each and 6
    T-shirts for $2.40 each. How much money did they spend?

    a. $5 \times \$8.95 + 6 \times 2.40$
    b. $(5 + 8.95) \times (6 + 2.40)$
    c. $(5 + 6) \times (8.95 + 2.40)$
    d. $(8.95 \div 5) + (2.40 \times 6)$
    e. $(8.95 + 2.40) \div (5 + 6)$

3. Katrina pays $99.90 for her monthly train pass. If she used
    her pass twice a day for 23 days last month, what was the
    average cost of each ride?

    a. $(99.90 \div 23) \times 2$
    b. $99.90 \div (23 \times 2)$
    c. $99.90 - (23 \times 2)$
    d. $99.90 \div 23$
    e. $99.90 \div 23 \times 2$

4. A coat normally selling for $80 was marked down 40%.
    What was the sale price?

    a. $80 - 40$
    b. $80 \div 40$
    c. $80 - .40 \times 80$
    d. $80 + .40 \times 80$
    e. $80 - 80 \div 40$

5. Dolores needs to buy eggs for the week. She will make six
    3-egg omelets for her family. She will also need 4 eggs for a
    cake and 2 eggs for a casserole. How many dozen eggs must
    she buy?

    a. $(6 \times 3) + 4 + 2$
    b. $(6 + 3 + 4 + 2) \div 12$
    c. $12 \times (6 \div 3) + (4 \div 2)$
    d. $6 \times 3 \div 12 + 4 + 2 \div 12$
    e. $(6 \times 3 + 4 + 2) \div 12$

Answers on page 184.

USING PICTURES OR DIAGRAMS TO SET UP MULTI-STEP WORD PROBLEMS

You can use pictures or diagrams to help you set up and solve multi-step word problems.

Example 1: Holly just moved into her new studio apartment. The main room is 30 feet long by 15 feet wide, and the bathroom is 9 feet long and 8 feet wide. What is the total size of her apartment in square feet?

Step 1: *question:* What is the total size of her apartment?

Step 2: *picture:*

Step 3: *set up:*

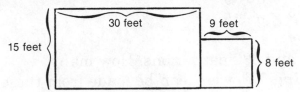

(30 feet × 15 feet) + (9 feet × 8 feet) = total size

Step 4: *solution:*

Multiply: 30 feet × 15 feet = 450 square feet

Multiply: 9 feet × 8 feet = 72 square feet

Add: 450 square feet + 72 square feet = **522 square feet**

Example 2: Donna's car gets 27 miles per gallon. After filling her 18-gallon gas tank, she drove 135 miles. How many more miles can she drive before her car runs out of gas?

Step 1: *question:* How many more miles?

Step 2: *diagram:*

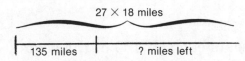

Step 3: *set up:*

(27 mpg × 18 gallons) − 135 miles = miles left

Step 4: *solution:*

Multiply: 27 mpg × 18 gallons = 486 miles

Subtract: 486 miles − 135 miles = **351 miles**

Exercise 6

For each word problem, draw a picture or diagram, and circle the letter of the correct setup.

1. A set of silverware included 8 place settings of a knife, fork, salad fork, teaspoon, and soupspoon as well as 6 serving pieces. How many pieces of silverware are in the set?

    diagram:
    - **a.** 8×6
    - **b.** $8 \times 6 - 5$
    - **c.** $8 \times 5 + 6$
    - **d.** $5 + 8 \times 6$
    - **e.** $8 \times 6 \div 5$

2. A florist has 420 roses and 380 carnations. How many bouquets, each containing 5 flowers, can be made from these flowers?

    diagram:
    - **a.** $(420 + 380) \times 5$
    - **b.** $5 \times 420 - 380$
    - **c.** $5 \div (420 + 380)$
    - **d.** $420 \times 5 - 380 \times 5$
    - **e.** $420 \div 5 + 380 \div 5$

3. Jan turned a 9-foot by 12-foot room in her home into an office. If she wants 3 equally sized bookcases along each of the 9-foot walls, how wide can each bookcase be?

    diagram:
    - **a.** $(9 \div 3) \times 2$
    - **b.** $(9 \times 12) \div 3$
    - **c.** $(9 \div 3) \times 12$
    - **d.** $9 \div 3$
    - **e.** $(12 \div 3) \times 9$

4. The theater has 30 rows of 25 seats each. If 150 of the seats are taken, how many are empty?

    diagram:
    - **a.** $(30 \times 25) - 150$
    - **b.** $(30 \times 25) \div 150$
    - **c.** $150 - 30 \times 25$
    - **d.** $(30 + 25) \times 150$
    - **e.** $(150 \div 30) + 25$

Answers on page 184.

SOLVING COMBINATION
WORD PROBLEMS INVOLVING CONVERSIONS

Many combination word problems involve conversions. To solve the following examples and problems, you should refer to the conversion chart on page 94. You should notice that a conversion is needed when 1 unit of measurement appears in the necessary information and a different unit of measurement is called for in the question.

Example 1: A dairy farm sold 156 <u>quarts</u> of milk at its own store and shipped out an additional 868 <u>quarts</u> to nearby supermarkets. How many <u>gallons</u> of milk were marketed?

Step 1: *question:* How many gallons of milk were marketed?

Step 2: *necessary information:* 156 quarts, 868 quarts

Step 3: *solution statement:*

$$\frac{\text{quarts}}{\text{gallon}} = \frac{\text{quarts}}{\text{gallon}}$$

$$\frac{4}{1} = \frac{\text{quarts}}{\text{gallons}}$$

There are 4 quarts in a gallon. This is written on the left side of the proportion as $\frac{4}{1}$.

$$\frac{4}{1} = \frac{1,024}{n}$$

missing information sentence:

$$4 \times n = 1 \times 1,024$$
$$4n = 1,024$$

quarts + quarts = total quarts
156 + 868 = 1,024 *quarts*

$$n = \frac{1,024}{4} = 256 \text{ gallons}$$

Step 4: Solve.

Example 2: A mill is cutting 8-<u>foot</u> lengths of lumber into chair legs. There are 6 <u>inches</u> of scrap for each length. What percent of the wood is scrap?

Step 1: *question:* What percent of the wood is scrap?

Step 2: *necessary information:* 8-foot, 6 inches

Step 3: *solution statement:*

$$\frac{\text{part}}{\text{whole}} = \frac{\text{percent}}{100}$$

$$\frac{6 \text{ inches}}{8 \text{ feet}} = \frac{n}{100}$$

Since all the information must be in the same unit of measurement, do the conversion.

conversion:

$$\frac{1 \; foot}{12 \; inches} = \frac{8 \; feet}{x}$$

$x = 12 \times 8$

$x = 96 \; inches$

Note: In the conversion, the letter x was used to stand for the unknown number of inches. Any letter can be used to stand for an unknown.

Step 4: Solve.

$$\frac{6 \; inches}{96 \; inches} = \frac{n}{100}$$
$$96n = 6 \times 100$$
$$96n = 600$$
$$n = \frac{600}{96} = 6\frac{1}{4}\%$$

• • • • • • • •
Exercise 7

Solve the following word problems, making the necessary conversions. Be careful; not all problems need a conversion.

1. Tile Town sells 81-square-inch tiles. How many tiles are needed to cover a 54-square-foot floor?

2. On the airplane assembly line, Isadore was able to make 20 welds an hour. How many welds did he make during a 9-hour workday?

3. On Interstate Highway, there is a reflector every 528 feet. How many reflectors are there on the stretch of highway shown at right?

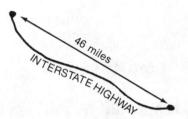

46 miles
INTERSTATE HIGHWAY

4. The medical center needed 48 gallons of blood after the earthquake. A nearby city donated 26 gallons of blood. The rest was donated at the medical center by people each giving 1 pint of blood. How many people gave a pint of blood at the center?

5. The Heat Coal Company distributed 38 tons of coal to its customers in 1 day. It delivered 400 pounds of coal to each of its customers. How many customers received deliveries?

6. Sharon was able to type 463 numbers during a 5-minute timing for data entry. At this rate, how many numbers could she type in an hour?

7. Lynn brought 12 quarts of ice cream to the Fourth of July picnic. If she gives each person a 4-ounce serving of ice cream, how many people will get the ice cream?

Answers on page 184.

SOLVING WORD PROBLEMS CONTAINING UNNECESSARY INFORMATION

Unnecessary information is more difficult to spot in combination word problems than in 1-step word problems. The key to identifying numbers as unnecessary is in working backward from the question. Once you write a word sentence, look at all the given information, and decide what is needed to answer the question.

Example 1: At sunrise, the temperature was 54 degrees. By mid-afternoon, it had risen 27 degrees. The temperature then began falling, until by midnight it had dropped 19 degrees from the high. What was the temperature at midafternoon?

Step 1: *question:* What was the temperature at midafternoon?

Step 2: *necessary information:* 54 degrees, 27 degrees (The fact that the temperature had dropped another 19 degrees by midnight is unnecessary information.)

Step 3: This is a 1-step problem. Write a word sentence: sunrise temperature + change = midafternoon temperature

Step 4: Solve:

$$54 + 27 = \textbf{81 degrees}$$

Example 2: A .8-ounce jar of basil sells for $.98. Marie plans to pack 3.5 pounds of basil into the jars. How many jars will she need?

Step 1: *question:* How many jars will she need?

Step 2: *necessary information:* .8 ounce, 3.5 pounds

(The cost of the jar of basil is unnecessary information.)

Step 3: *solution proportion:*

$$\frac{\text{total weight}}{\text{number of jars}} = \frac{\text{weight}}{1 \text{ jar}}$$

Since all your weights must be in the same unit of measurement, your next step must be a conversion to find the number of ounces in a pound.

$$\text{conversion:} \quad \frac{16 \text{ ounces}}{1 \text{ pound}} = \frac{n \text{ ounces}}{3.5 \text{ pounds}}$$

$$1 \times n = 3.5 \times 16$$

$$n = 56 \text{ ounces}$$

Step 4: Solve.

$$\frac{3.5 \text{ pounds}}{n \text{ jars}} = \frac{.8 \text{ ounce}}{1 \text{ jar}}$$

$$\frac{56 \text{ ounces}}{n \text{ jars}} = \frac{.8 \text{ ounce}}{1 \text{ jar}}$$

$$.8 \times n = 56 \times 1$$

$$.8n = 56$$

$$n = \frac{56}{.8} = 70 \text{ jars}$$

• • • • • • • •
Exercise 8

Write the word sentences or proportion needed to solve the following word problems. Underline the necessary information. Then solve the problem. Be careful; many of these problems contain unnecessary information.

1. At the beginning of the school year, the Philadelphia school system had 103,912 students. During the course of the year, 4,657 students left the system, while 1,288 more students were enrolled. What was the student population at the end of the year?

2. At the beginning of the school year, the Philadelphia school system had 103,912 students. During the course of the year, 4,657 students left the system, while 1,288 more students were enrolled. How many different students spent at least part of the year in the Philadelphia school system?

3. At sunrise, the temperature was 54 degrees. By midafternoon, it had risen 27 degrees. The temperature then began falling, until by midnight it had dropped 19 degrees from the high. What was the temperature at midnight?

4. Every week, after having $53 taken out of his paycheck, Lloyd takes home $148. What was Lloyd's take-home pay for a 52-week year?

5. Ahmed bought 3 paperbacks and 2 magazines at the drugstore at the prices shown at right. He paid for his purchases with a $20 bill. How much change did he receive at the drugstore?

Hoyle's Drugstore
Newspapers—$.35
Paperbacks—$2.95
Magazines—$1.50
Postcards—$.23

6. Sangita is a member of a cooperative grocery store. She gets a 20% discount off everything she buys in the store. She bought a 5-pound bag of oranges marked $1.65. After receiving her discount, how much did she pay for the oranges?

Answers on page 185.

SOLVING LONGER COMBINATION WORD PROBLEMS

Sometimes word problems cannot be solved by being broken into two 1-step problems. 3 or more steps may be needed to solve the problem. The method used with these problems is the same as the method used throughout this chapter with combination word problems. Keep working backward from the question. Set up a solution sentence, and solve shorter problems to get all of the information that you need.

Example: Sylvia went shopping in the bargain basement. She bought a $24.99 dress marked $\frac{1}{3}$ off and a $16.95 pair of pants marked down 20%. How much did she spend?

Step 1: *question:* How much did she spend?

Step 2: *necessary information:* $24.99, $\frac{1}{3}$ off; $16.95, marked down 20%

Step 3: *solution sentence:*

dress price + pants price = total spent

To solve this, you must find the sale prices of both the dress and the pants. Both can be found by using this *missing information* sentence:

original price − discount amount = sale price

You can find the discount by multiplying the original amount by a fraction or percent.

dress
$24.99 − ($\frac{1}{3}$ × 24.99) = *sale price*
  24.99 − 8.33 = $16.66

pants
$16.95 − (20% of 16.95) = *sale price*
  16.95 − (.20 × 16.95) = *sale price*
  16.95 − 3.39 = $13.56

Step 4: Solve.

$16.66 + $13.56 = **$30.22**

Note: Chapter 9 used the proportion method for solving percent word problems. However, if a problem requires you to find a percent of an amount, there is another method. Simply change the percent to a decimal, and multiply. In the example above, 20% was changed to .20.

● ● ● ● ● ● ● ●
Exercise 9

For every problem, write all necessary word sentences or
proportions. Then solve the problem. Round off money solutions
to the nearest penny.

1. Kerry bought 7 apples and a cantaloupe at the prices
    shown at right. How much did she spend?

Cantaloupe	$.88 each
Grapes	$1.39 per pound
Apples	$1.56 per dozen

    _____

2. Aaron received a gas bill of $36.80 for 32 gallons of bottled
    gas. If he pays the bill within 10 days, he will receive a 6%
    discount. How much will he have to pay if he pays his bill
    within 10 days?

    _____

3. Harold's doctor advised him to cut down on the calories he
    consumed by 28%. Harold had been consuming 4,200
    calories a day. If Harold's breakfast contains 797 calories,
    how many calories can he have during the rest of the day?

    _____

4. Sarkis is a salesman. He receives a salary of $70 a week
    plus a 6% commission on all his sales over $200. Last week,
    he sold $1,160 worth of merchandise. What was he paid for
    the week?

    _____

5. Dinora drove 3,627 miles from coast to coast. Her car
    averaged 31 miles per gallon, and she spent $186 for gas.
    On the average, what did she pay per gallon of gas?

    _____

Answers on page 185.

REVIEW: SOLVING COMBINATION WORD PROBLEMS

. . . .
Exercise 10

For all problems, choose the 1 best answer. Round off decimals to the nearest penny or the nearest hundredth.

1. Every day, Kevin has to drive 7 miles each way to work and back. At work, he has to drive his truck on a 296-mile delivery route. How many miles does he drive during a 5-day workweek?

    a. *310 miles*
    b. *315 miles*
    c. *1,550 miles*
    d. *4,214 miles*
    e. *none of the above*

2. Every day, Jason has a 14-mile round-trip drive to work. He then has to drive his truck on a 296-mile delivery route 5 days a week. How many miles does he drive each day?

    a. *310 miles*
    b. *315 miles*
    c. *1,550 miles*
    d. *4,214 miles*
    e. *none of the above*

3. For his art class, Karl spent $135 on books and $225 on materials. To cover costs, how much did each of his 15 students have to pay?

    a. *$360*
    b. *$90*
    c. *$24*
    d. *$15*
    e. *$9*

4. Jessie's restaurant had 4 small dining rooms with a capacity of 28 people each and a main dining room with a capacity of 94 people. What was the total capacity of the restaurant?

    a. *126 people*
    b. *658 people*
    c. *348 people*
    d. *122 people*
    e. *206 people*

5. Each team in the 8-team football league used to have a roster of 36 players. The league decided to decrease each team's roster size by 3 players. Before the change, how many players were in the league?

   a. *180 players*
   b. *288 players*
   c. *285 players*
   d. *264 players*
   e. *396 players*

6. Each team in the 8-team football league used to have a roster of 36 players. The league decided to decrease each team's roster size by 3 players. After the change, how many players were in the league?

   a. *180 players*
   b. *288 players*
   c. *285 players*
   d. *264 players*
   e. *396 players*

7. At the supermarket, Monique bought 2.36 pounds of cheese and 4 pounds of apples. What was the total cost of the cheese and apples at the prices shown at right?

   a. *$7.48*
   b. *$4.43*
   c. *$3.94*
   d. *$5.69*
   e. *$4.29*

   **Meg's Market
   on Sale This Week!**

   Apples—only $.49/pound
   Chicken—only $1.39/pound
   Potato Salad—only $.79/pint
   Cheese—only $1.58/pound
   ---

8. A bottle contains 6 cups of laundry detergent. The directions say to use $\frac{1}{3}$ cup for a top-loading washer and $\frac{1}{4}$ cup for a front-loading washer. How many more loads per bottle can you do with a front-loading washer than with a top-loading washer?

   a. *1 load*
   b. *3 loads*
   c. *6 loads*
   d. *8 loads*
   e. *9 loads*

Answers on page 185.

Post-Tests

POST-TEST A

For all problems, choose the correct answer. Round off decimals to the nearest penny or the nearest hundredth.

1. 3 tablespoons cocoa plus 1 tablespoon fat can be substituted for 1 ounce chocolate in baking recipes. A recipe for chocolate cake calls for 12 ounces of chocolate. If Shirley is substituting cocoa for chocolate, how much cocoa should she use?

   a. *15 tablespoons*
   b. *9 tablespoons*
   c. *4 tablespoons*
   d. *36 tablespoons*
   e. *17 tablespoons*

2. Matt has a 400-square-inch board. He needs a 25-square-inch piece of the board for the floor of a birdhouse. What percent of the board will he need for the floor of the birdhouse?

   a. *425 square inches*
   b. *375 square inches*
   c. *$6\frac{1}{4}\%$*
   d. *$93\frac{3}{4}\%$*
   e. *100%*

3. There are 5,372 school-age children in town. 1,547 either go to private school or have dropped out. How many children remain in the town's public schools?

   a. *6,919 children*
   b. *3,825 children*
   c. *4,235 children*
   d. *4,839 children*
   e. *none of the above*

4. A bushel of apples weighs 48 pounds. Tanya wants to buy
    12 pounds of apples. How many bushels should she buy?

    a. *4 bushels*
    b. *36 bushels*
    c. *$\frac{1}{2}$ bushel*
    d. *$\frac{1}{4}$ bushel*
    e. *none of the above*

5. At the sidewalk stand, Jason bought a hot dog and a soda.
    How much did he spend at the prices shown at right?

    a. *$1.95*
    b. *$2.00*
    c. *$.65*
    d. *$84.50*
    e. *$.02*

6. If Kenneth retires at age 65, he will receive as a pension
    80% of his salary of $18,657. If he retires at age 62, he will
    receive only 70% of his salary. How much smaller will his
    pension be if he retires early?

    a. *$1,865.70*
    b. *$10*
    c. *$18,507*
    d. *$3,331.41*
    e. *$13,059.90*

7. 1 cup sugar plus $\frac{1}{4}$ cup liquid can be substituted for 1 cup
    corn syrup in baking recipes. A recipe calls for $1\frac{1}{2}$ cups
    corn syrup. If Mira is substituting sugar for corn syrup,
    how much liquid should she add?

    a. *$\frac{3}{8}$ cup*
    b. *$\frac{1}{6}$ cup*
    c. *6 cups*
    d. *$1\frac{1}{4}$ cups*
    e. *$3\frac{3}{4}$ cups*

8. A conservation organization charged each member $10
    dues plus $5 for the organization's magazine. How much
    money did the organization collect from its 13,819
    members?

    a. *$207,285*
    b. *$138,190*

    c. $69,095

    d. $690,950

    e. $138,195

9. Pat and Connie are able to put down $16,000 as a down payment on a new home. Their bank told them that they must pay at least 8% of the purchase price as a down payment. What is the most expensive home they can afford?

    a. $128,000

    b. $16,008

    c. $96,000

    d. $15,992

    e. $200,000

10. For her wardrobe, Mrs. Are was given a Paris original worth $1,346, a New York original worth $658, and a Goodwill original worth $4. What was the total value of the clothes given to her?

    a. $2,008

    b. $692

    c. $501

    d. $684

    e. $8,016

11. After 3 years, Elsie's car had lost $\frac{1}{3}$ of its original value. 2 years later, it had lost an additional $\frac{1}{4}$ of its original value. If she bought the car for $3,600, what was it worth after 5 years?

    a. $4,800

    b. $2,700

    c. $3,300

    d. $2,100

    e. $1,500

12. There are 3 feet in a yard. There are 1,760 yards in a mile. How many feet long is the Walk for Peace shown at right?

    a. 15 feet

    b. 2,935$\frac{2}{3}$ feet

    c. 26,400 feet

    d. 8,800 feet

    e. 5,280 feet

WALK FOR PEACE MAY 5TH 5 MILES

13. Lorraine weighed $172\frac{1}{2}$ pounds. She lost $47\frac{3}{4}$ pounds in one year. What was her new weight?

   a. *$219\frac{1}{4}$ pounds*
   b. *$118\frac{3}{4}$ pounds*
   c. *$124\frac{3}{4}$ pounds*
   d. *$125\frac{1}{4}$ pounds*
   e. *none of the above*

14. To qualify for the car race, Christine needed to drive 100 miles in under 43 minutes. She completed the first lap in $4\frac{1}{2}$ minutes. At this rate, what will be her total time for the 100-mile qualifying distance?

   a. *41 minutes*
   b. *45 minutes*
   c. *$193\frac{1}{2}$ minutes*
   d. *$47\frac{1}{2}$ minutes*
   e. *not enough information is given*

15. Nickilena, Jean, Rosemary, and Elaine went into business together. The 4-woman partnership earned $36,460 and had expenses of $23,188. If they split the profits evenly, how much did each woman make?

   a. *$5,797*
   b. *$3,318*
   c. *$14,912*
   d. *$9,115*
   e. *$14,073*

16. Sears is offering 20% off on its $260 refrigerator. How much can you save by buying the refrigerator on sale?

   a. *$52*
   b. *$202*
   c. *$312*
   d. *$104*
   e. *none of the above*

17. $\frac{1}{3}$ of the voters polled said they were planning to vote for the incumbent, while $\frac{1}{4}$ said they were planning to vote for the challenger. The rest were undecided. What fraction of the voters had decided which way they were going to vote?

    a. $\frac{2}{7}$

    b. $\frac{1}{12}$

    c. $\frac{3}{4}$

    d. $\frac{7}{12}$

    e. $1\frac{1}{3}$

18. Denise is paid $7.20 per hour at her part-time job. Last week she worked 17.5 hours. How much did she earn last week at her part-time job?

    a. *$24.70*

    b. *$126.00*

    c. *$2.43*

    d. *$10.30*

    e. *not enough information is given*

19. Jane bought the new hatchback automobile pictured at right. She ordered $435 of added options and received a $650 rebate. How much did Jane pay for the car?

$6,578

    a. *$7,663*

    b. *$7,013*

    c. *$7,228*

    d. *$5,493*

    e. *$6,363*

20. East Somerville has 948 homes. 12 people are collecting money for the Heart Association. If they all visit the same number of homes, how many homes should each of them visit?

    a. *960 homes*

    b. *936 homes*

    c. *79 homes*

    d. *11,376 homes*

    e. *none of the above*

21. Melvin received an electric bill for $86.29. He knows that it cost him $59 a month for his air-conditioning. How much would his bill have been if he had not operated the air conditioner?

    a. *$155.29*
    b. *$27.29*
    c. *$50.91*
    d. *$14.63*
    e. *none of the above*

22. Eileen bought 3 pairs of socks for $1.79 each and 4 towels for $2.69 each. How much did she spend?

    a. *$4.48*
    b. *$11.48*
    c. *$31.36*
    d. *$16.13*
    e. *$7.00*

23. Steve's Ice Cream Store puts $\frac{1}{16}$ pound of whipped cream on every sundae. For how many sundaes will the container of whipped cream pictured at right last?

    a. *25 sundaes*
    b. *7 sundaes*
    c. *144 sundaes*
    d. *26 sundaes*
    e. *none of the above*

24. After paying $14.43 for dinner and $3.50 for a movie, Florence paid the baby-sitter $5.00. How much did the evening cost her?

    a. *$12.93*
    b. *$22.93*
    c. *$5.93*
    d. *$8.50*
    e. *$19.43*

25. A pile of books weighed 34.2 pounds. If each book weighed .6 pound, how many books were in the pile?

    a. *35 books*
    b. *34 books*
    c. *21 books*
    d. *20 books*
    e. *57 books*

Answers on page 186.

POST-TEST B

For all problems, circle the letter of the correct answer. Round off decimals to the nearest penny or the nearest hundredth.

1. Large eggs weigh $1\frac{1}{2}$ pounds per dozen. Dawn bought 8 large eggs. How much did the eggs weigh?

   a. *3 ounces*
   b. *$\frac{1}{3}$ pound*
   c. *1 pound*
   d. *18 ounces*
   e. *not enough information is given*

2. Glenn, the owner of a hardware store, originally paid $540.60 for 15 tool sets. At his year-end clearance sale, he sold the last tool set for $24.00. How much money did he lose on the last tool set?

   a. *$180.60*
   b. *$1.50*
   c. *$12.04*
   d. *$36.04*
   e. *none of the above*

3. Manny was working as a hot dog vendor. He sold a total of 426 hot dogs in one weekend. If he sold 198 on Saturday, how many did he sell on Sunday?

   a. *624 hot dogs*
   b. *332 hot dogs*
   c. *228 hot dogs*
   d. *514 hot dogs*
   e. *none of the above*

4. The television announcer reported that Elizabeth Quezada had received 39% of the votes in the race for mayor. The totals board behind the announcer showed that Elizabeth had received 156,000 votes. How many votes were cast in the election?

   a. *40,000 votes*
   b. *400,000 votes*
   c. *156,039 votes*
   d. *608,480 votes*
   e. *60,840 votes*

5. On the average, Kennedy Airport has 96 jumbo jets arriving each day. Each jumbo jet has an average of 214 passengers. How many passengers arrive by jumbo jet at Kennedy Airport each day?

   a. *310 passengers*
   b. *20,544 passengers*
   c. *118 passengers*
   d. *222 passengers*
   e. *none of the above*

6. To finish off the room, Ed needs a tile only $\frac{1}{3}$ foot wide. How much did he have to cut off the tile pictured at right so that it would fit?

   a. $\frac{1}{2}$ *foot*
   b. $\frac{5}{12}$ *foot*
   c. $\frac{4}{7}$ *foot*
   d. $\frac{1}{4}$ *foot*
   e. $\frac{4}{9}$ *foot*

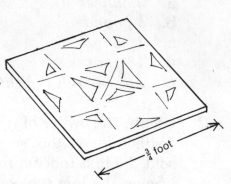
$\frac{3}{4}$ foot

7. After picking a bushel of apples, Tina planned to divide the apples evenly among herself and 5 of her neighbors. How many apples did each of them get if the bushel weighed 54 pounds?

   a. *9 apples*
   b. *60 apples*
   c. *48 apples*
   d. *324 apples*
   e. *not enough information is given*

8. 1.23 cubic yards of concrete are needed to cover 100 square feet with 4 inches of concrete. How many cubic yards are needed to cover 550 square feet with 4 inches of concrete?

   a. *650 square feet*
   b. *4.92 cubic yards*
   c. *6.77 cubic yards*
   d. *2,200 square inches*
   e. *27.06 cubic yards*

9. Pedro needs 4 pounds of hamburger for his chili recipe. In his freezer, he had a 2.64-pound package of hamburger. How much more hamburger did he need?

   a. *6.64 pounds*
   b. *2.68 pounds*
   c. *1.36 pounds*
   d. *1.52 pounds*
   e. *10.56 pounds*

10. Last year, the city's supermarkets sold 1,638,000 gallons of milk. There are 78,000 people in the city. On the average, how many gallons of milk did each person buy?

    a. *1,716,000 gallons*
    b. *1,560,000 gallons*
    c. *21 gallons*
    d. *127,716 million gallons*
    e. *not enough information is given*

11. After having $48.23 taken out of his paycheck, Maurice takes home $132.77 every week. What are Maurice's total gross earnings for a 52-week year?

    a. *$4,396.08*
    b. *$9,412.00*
    c. *$8,814.90*
    d. *$6,904.04*
    e. *$2,507.96*

12. 423 service stations in the state closed in the last year. Only 2,135 remain. How many service stations existed in the state a year ago?

    a. *2,558 service stations*
    b. *1,712 service stations*
    c. *2,312 service stations*
    d. *2,512 service stations*
    e. *none of the above*

13. A $\frac{2}{3}$ majority of those voting in the House of
Representatives is needed to override a presidential veto. If
all 435 representatives vote, how many votes are needed to
override a veto?

   a. 290 votes
   b. 145 votes
   c. 657 votes
   d. 658 votes
   e. 224 votes

14. Naomi had $61 in her checking account. She wrote a check
for $28 and made a $115 deposit. How much money did she
then have in the account?

   a. $204
   b. $24
   c. $148
   d. $82
   e. $34

15. Avi needed to replace the molding on the left side of his car
after it was damaged. The door needed $33\frac{3}{4}$ inches of
molding, while the rear quarter panel needed $51\frac{2}{3}$ inches.
How many inches of molding did he need if he replaced the
molding on the door and the rear quarter panel?

   a. $2247\frac{5}{12}$ inches
   b. $85\frac{5}{12}$ inches
   c. $17\frac{11}{12}$ inches
   d. $\frac{87}{124}$ inch
   e. $\frac{124}{87}$ inches

16. Ben, who works at the meat counter at the local
supermarket, had to price the meat yesterday because the
machine that normally did the job was broken. What price
should he put on a 2.64-pound rib roast selling at $3.96 a
pound?

   a. $1.50
   b. $5.94
   c. $6.60
   d. $10.45
   e. $1.32

17. 28% of the workers at the factory were women. There were 432 male workers. What was the total number of workers at the factory?

    a. *460 workers*
    b. *12,096 workers*
    c. *600 workers*
    d. *1,543 workers*
    e. *404 workers*

18. Sarah bought the carton of nails pictured at right. How much did each nail weigh?

    a. *56 pounds*
    b. *100 pounds*
    c. *.01 pound*
    d. $\frac{1}{56}$ *pound*
    e. $\frac{3}{100}$ *pound*

19. In the first quarter, the Philadelphia 76ers hit only 7 out of 25 field goal attempts. What was their scoring percentage?

    a. *28%*
    b. *32%*
    c. *72%*
    d. *76%*
    e. *18%*

20. Carla gained 3 pounds in the first month of her new diet and 4 pounds in the second month. Her original weight was 104 pounds. What was her new weight?

    a. *97 pounds*
    b. *105 pounds*
    c. *103 pounds*
    d. *111 pounds*
    e. *100 pounds*

21. Peg bought the roast and the steak shown at right. How much meat did she buy?

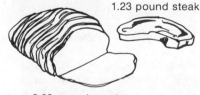

1.23 pound steak

3.69 pound roast

    a. *4.92 pounds*
    b. *3 pounds*
    c. *4.54 pounds*
    d. *2.46 pounds*
    e. *.33 pound*

22.   Glennie had $74.81 in her checking account. She wrote
       checks for $46.19 and $22.45. She then made a $60.00
       deposit. What was her new balance?

       a. $203.45
       b. $66.17
       c. $83.45
       d. $53.83
       e. $38.55

23.   Premium Ice Cream is 9% milkfat. How many pounds of
       milkfat are in a 450-pound batch of Premium Ice Cream?

       a.   50 pounds
       b.   441 pounds
       c.   459 pounds
       d.   40.5 pounds
       e.   2 pounds

24.   At the start of a trip, Tony filled his gas tank. After
       driving 168 miles, he needed 5.6 gallons of gasoline to fill
       his tank. How many gallons of gasoline would he use for
       the 417-mile drive from his home to his brother's home?

       a.   44.5 gallons
       b.   13.9 gallons
       c.   74.5 gallons
       d.   8.3 gallons
       e.   19.5 gallons

25.   A piece of cheese was labeled $1.79 a pound. The price of
       the cheese was $1.06. How much did the cheese weigh?

       a. $2.85
       b. $.73
       c.   1.69 pounds
       d.   1.90 pounds
       e.   .59 pound

Answers on page 187.